# NATURE'S WORKSHOP

## Crafts for every season

by Pernelle Sévy

translated by Laurence and Rona Wood
photographs by François Cherrier

Angus & Robertson · Publishers

# Contents

**GOING METRIC**

In this book you will find two systems of measurement.
The first set of figures refer to the metric system and
the second to the imperial. Wherever possible both sets
of measurements have been worked out in round
numbers, but remember that this means that the metric
and imperial are not equivalent, so make sure you only
work with one set of figures.

Angus & Robertson · Publishers
London · Sydney · Melbourne · Singapore
Manila

Copyright © Librairie Hachette, 1974
Text of this edition copyright ©
Angus & Robertson (U.K.) Ltd. 1976

ISBN 0 207 95677 4

Made and printed in Italy
by New Interlitho, Milan.

Tain Guide Hut

donated by

Heather McAllister

Aug '89

# Introduction

Flowers and fruit, leaves and seeds, shells and stones are all yours to collect and enjoy. Without spoiling the countryside you can find many raw materials for creating lovely things. If you know where to look, each season of the year provides different treasures:

In spring you can fill the house with wild flowers, or press them; find pebbles in streams and make primitive jewellery . . .

In summer you can collect shells, leaves and ears of corn— they have endless decorative uses; or you can make colour slides from seaweed . . .

Autumn brings a harvest of seeds, russet leaves, gourds and dried flowers from which you can make pictures, panels and greetings cards . . .

Winter is the time for constructing strange animals, puppets and party candles.

These are just a few of the fascinating things to be found in the countryside and on the seashore. If you add to these some common garden plants and certain seeds that you can buy from a grocer or supermarket, you can make up a magnificent collection of materials. This book will tell you where to find them and how to preserve them, and will give you lots of ideas for using them in exciting ways.

| | | |
|---|---|---|
| 1 knife | 7 glue brush | 13 gouge |
| 2 scissors | 8 tube of glue | 14 tweezers |
| 3 pins, needles, thread | 9 pot of adhesive | 15 string |
| 4 bradawl | 10 gouache | 16 thread |
| 5 hammer | 11 leather punch for large holes | 17 clear adhesive |
| 6 water colour brush | 12 leather punch for small holes | 18 gimlet |

| Adhesives | How to use them | Where to buy them |
|---|---|---|
| Slow-drying adhesives (cellulose adhesives, wall-paper pastes). | Use a flat brush. Suitable for paper, card and cloth. Wash the brush after use. | A, C, D, E |
| Adhesives for delicate materials, such as leaves, flowers, seaweeds (e.g. Copydex). | Use from the tube. You can move the object around while it is drying. Rub away any superfluous adhesive when dry. | A, B |
| Quick-drying adhesives. | Use from the tube. Aerosol adhesives should be used only for large areas, and never for cloth. | A, B, D, E, F |
| Super-quick-drying adhesives (e.g. Uhu). | Use from the tube. Hold the parts together till dry. | A, B, D, E, F |
| Tough adhesives for hard materials (e.g. Araldite and wood glues). | Follow instructions carefully—the adhesive must not be too cold. Fix the objects firmly in place. | D, E, F |
| Modelling clay. No firing necessary. | Use with objects without flat surfaces (e.g. shells). Knead with your fingers till soft. | A, B |

| Colours | How to use them | Where to buy them |
|---|---|---|
| Ordinary gouache. | Use a pointed water colour brush, and only on objects which tolerate damp. | A, B, E |
| Acrylic gouache. | Dilute slightly with water. Clean brushes well. Indelible when dry. | A, B |
| Metallized paints (e.g. Humbrol). | Use a brush or aerosol depending on area to be covered. Clean brushes with the solvent recommended. | A, D, F |
| Coloured inks. | Use a pointed brush. The inks are transparent and their colours will blend with those of the object painted (e.g. shells, seeds). | A, B, E |
| Leather dye. | Use a soft brush. | D, E, G |

A. Stationers
B. Artists' suppliers
C. Home decorating
D. Ironmongers
E. Department stores
F. Model and toy shops
G. Shoe shops and shoe repairers

**Things to gather in spring**

Flowers, foliage, plants, stones (minerals, pebbles, etc.), driftwood, roots, snails.

**Lay in reserves for later on.** All kinds of flowers and leaves.

spring

# Arranging flowers

**Materials.** Wild or garden flowers, leaves, anything you can use as a vase, basket or plastic bag, knife and secateurs, scissors, wire netting (a piece three times the size of the neck of your vase), cutting pliers, pin-holders, floral wax or plasticine, synthetic moss (optional).

A beautiful flower arrangement doesn't need to be expensive. You can make one with wild flowers if you know how to use them.

**Picking.** If you pick your flowers in the morning when the stalks are full of sap, they will still be fresh when you get them home. Choose flowers which are just opening, as buds often fail to open. Flowers with powdery stamens die quickly, since they are already fertilized. Daffodils and other bulbs can be picked in bud – they will flower in water. Leaves and shoots are decorative too, but remember to cut twigs with care, so as not to damage young trees.

Never carry flowers in your warm hand, as this will make them wilt: use a basket or plastic bag. Cut long stalks, but don't uproot plants. Some flowers are becoming rare and should be protected. Only pick the ones you really need and leave the others growing.

**Preparation.** When you get home put all the flowers in a deep bowl or bucket, immerse the stalks in water and let them drink. Then remove the lowest leaves from each stalk (if leaves are under water they will rot in the vase), and cut the end of the stalk off *under water* to prevent a bubble of air blocking the water supply to the flower. Now choose a vase – something in keeping with the flowers, and the right size to support them if you have no flower-holder. Any container will do, from a jam-pot to a casserole. Fill it with clean water (rainwater if possible) and put in half an aspirin to keep it fresh.

**Aids.** Flowers with a lot of foliage are easy to arrange, but for others a flower-holder is useful:

Wire netting, bent to a bowl-shape to fit the vase (fig. 1). Cut the wire with pliers and bend the ends over the edge. The flowers will hide the ends.

A pin-holder, round or square, on which to fix the stalks. Put it in the bottom of the vase, and stick it down with plasticine if necessary (fig. 2).

Artificial moss makes it possible to use any kind of shallow container. One variety (Oasis) can be cut to size, while another (Florapak) can be shaped in water. After it has been thoroughly soaked, the flower stalks can be stuck directly into it (fig. 3).

fig. 1    fig. 2    fig. 3    fig. 4

**Arrangement.** The only firm rule in creative arrangement is to make a balanced composition of colours and shapes. The general shape will depend on where you are going to put it – it should be rounded for a low table, two-dimensional if it is to go against a wall, or low for the centre of a dining-table. Its shape will also depend on the container and the kind of flowers you use (figs 4–9). Above all, try to keep it natural-looking.

**Looking after the flowers.** Add a little water to the vase or moss every day. If the room is very warm, put in an ice cube. It is a good idea to sprinkle the flowers themselves. At night the vase can be moved to a cooler place – but keep it out of draughts.

fig. 5

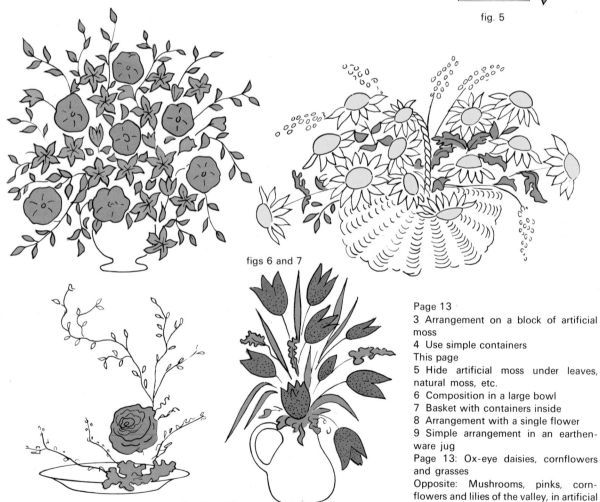

figs 6 and 7

figs 8 and 9

Page 13
3 Arrangement on a block of artificial moss
4 Use simple containers
This page
5 Hide artificial moss under leaves, natural moss, etc.
6 Composition in a large bowl
7 Basket with containers inside
8 Arrangement with a single flower
9 Simple arrangement in an earthenware jug
Page 13: Ox-eye daisies, cornflowers and grasses
Opposite: Mushrooms, pinks, cornflowers and lilies of the valley, in artificial moss, with other flowers and grasses

Family: *Labiatae*
Name: *Lavandula sp.*
Picked: August, garden

# Herbarium

**Materials**. Pocket guide to wild flowers, box or plastic bag, knife, old newspapers, sheets of drawing paper about 35 × 25 cm/14 × 10″ (one for each plant), scissors, stick-on labels, clear adhesive tape, paste.

You will learn a lot in making a herbarium and it will not cost you anything but time and a little patience.

**Collecting**. With small plants (unless they are rare ones) take the root as well, otherwise take part of the main stem. Pick one or two specimens of each type when they are in full flower. Put them in a plastic bag or oblong box, but don't over-crowd them. Don't leave them too long, or they will dry out.

**Identification**. This will be easier when the plants are still fresh. Consult your wild flower guide.

**Drying**. Dry the plants between sheets of white blotting paper. Be careful to spread out the petals and leaves first — this will be impossible to do after drying, as they will be very brittle. Put some heavy books on top of the paper and leave to dry for several days. Some juicy plants may even need a few weeks.

**Arranging the herbarium**. Lay the pressed plants, well spaced out, on the drawing paper and fix them down with small strips of clear adhesive tape about 3 mm/⅛″ wide, put crosswise over the main and side stems. In the case of trees, don't forget to stick down a small piece of bark as well as a leaf and perhaps a flower.

In one corner of the paper stick a label containing the species of plant, its Latin and common names, and the place and date of picking. You can also add a photograph or drawing to make it decorative as well as interesting.

Family: *Liliaceae*
Name: *Fritillaria meleagris* (snake's head)
:ked: May, Oxfordshire, water meadow

Family: *Geraniaceae*
Name: *Geranium lucidum L.* (shining cranesbill)
Picked: June, Sussex, shady bank

Family: *Ranunculaceae*
Name: *Helleborus corsicus* (Corsican hellebore)
Picked: May, Hampshire, garden

17

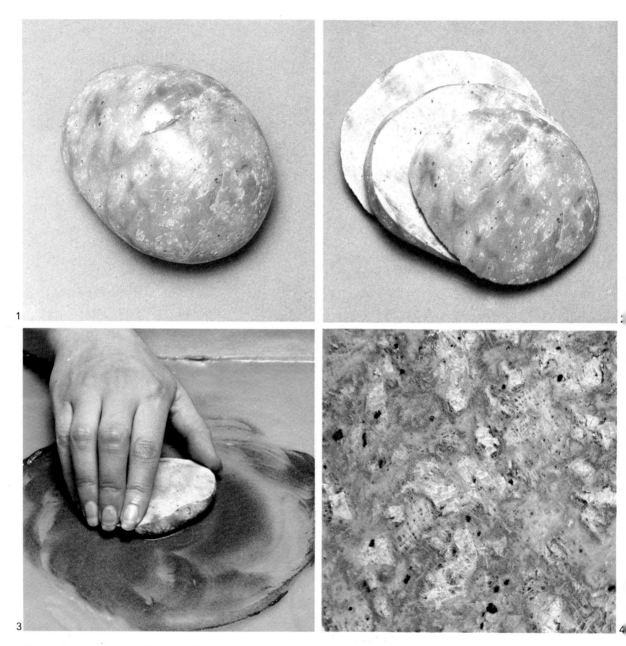

# Rocks and minerals

**Materials.** Geologist's hammer and chisel, bag (preferably one you can sling on your back, like a rucksack), sheets of newspaper, magnifying glass, handbook for identifying specimens, Indian ink, notebook.

When you pick up stones on your walks you always hope to find something like a fossil amongst them — but even if you don't there are plenty of beautiful stones, even among the common ones. By studying them you can learn a lot about the history of the earth.

**Collecting.** It's a good idea to find out something about the area you are in so that you know the best places to head for. You are most likely to find good specimens where the ground has been cut vertically – either by natural river banks or escarpments or by man-made railway cuttings, roads and quarries. If you choose a quarry, get permission first from the owners, and make sure there is no danger from falling rocks. Travel light, because you may be weighed down with stones on the way home. You may pick up isolated specimens, but often you will have to break pieces off with your hammer and chisel. If the rock is friable or fragile (for example pegmatite or foliated talc) wrap each piece in newspaper. Seaside pebbles are often interesting, but they will not necessarily merit a place in your rock collection.

**Identification.** There are many handbooks giving descriptions and photographs of the commoner rocks and minerals. You must judge the physical character of your specimen – hardness, and the way it fractures (use a magnifying glass for this). Other tests – chemical or electromagnetic – are needed to identify some types of rocks, but it will be easier for you to go to a local museum and compare your rocks with theirs.

**Arrangement.** Don't stick labels on your specimens. Write a number on each piece with Indian ink, and against the same number in your notebook write the name of the rock and the place where you found it. It is best to keep your specimens in a glass case to keep dust out. Some rocks look best polished or fixed on a base.

## Polishing

**Materials.** Small electric grinder and polisher, with accessories, or alternatively a sheet of plate glass 6 mm/$\frac{1}{4}$″ thick, 20 × 30 cm/8 × 12″, silicon carbide grit or paper (nos. 320, 400, 600), piece of leather 15 cm/6″ square, tin oxide powder, thick gloves.

**Method.** Two operations are required – grinding (with silicon carbide) and polishing (with tin oxide). Always wear gloves to protect you against the heat created by friction and accidental contact with the wheel which can be very painful. It is best if an adult supervises work done on electric polishers and grinders, since accidents can happen.

You can use a small electric grinder placed under a tap so that water drips on the wheel, which must be kept wet. For hard stones use a cast iron wheel. Cover the surface to be ground with silicon carbide and

hold the stone firmly against the wheel. For softer stones use a wooden wheel or leather belt. After grinding carefully, put a felt disc on the motor and finish by polishing with tin oxide, holding the stone as before.

If you have no grinding machine you can get a monumental mason to cut your stones into slices, and you can polish these by hand. Spread silicon carbide on a sheet of plate glass, mix it with a little water, and rub the slice of stone on the glass until the surface is smooth (page 18, figs 3 and 4). Alternatively you can use silicon carbide paper as used on car bodies. The paper has different numbers according to the size of the grit, and is used wet. Start with the coarsest, no. 300, and then continue with no. 400. When the stone is smooth use no. 600. You will obtain an even smoother surface, ready for polishing.

For polishing use a leather square, preferably glued to a piece of wood to keep it firm. Make a paste of tin oxide and water, spread it on the leather and rub your stone hard on it. All these operations take time and patience, and seem rather monotonous. Try watching television or reading a book while you work.

## Mounting pebble sections on a base

**Materials.** Pebble section (the one shown on page 19 is 8.5 × 9.5 × 0 .5 cm/$3\frac{1}{2}$ × 4 × $\frac{3}{16}$″), block of wood 6.5 × 3.5 × 3.5 cm/$2\frac{1}{2}$ × $1\frac{1}{2}$ × $1\frac{1}{2}$″, gouge, Araldite (optional), wood stain, wax.

**Method.** Gouge out a hole in the upper surface of the wood block, as in fig. 1, so that its width corresponds exactly with the thickness of the pebble section. If you cut down to about 8 mm/$\frac{3}{8}$″ the stone will stand straight in the hole. You can fix it with Araldite. Colour the wood if you wish, using a wood stain, as in the photograph on page 19.

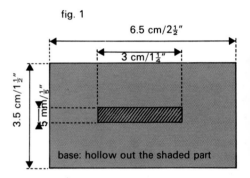

fig. 1

6.5 cm/$2\frac{1}{2}$″

3 cm/$1\frac{1}{4}$″

3.5 cm/$1\frac{1}{2}$″

5 mm/$\frac{1}{5}$″

base: hollow out the shaded part

## Abstract sculpture on a base

**Materials.** Pieces of rock, wooden base, iron or brass rods 2.5 mm/$\frac{1}{10}$″ in diameter the actual length depending on size of your stones, hacksaw, electric or hand drill, tungsten carbide bit 2.5 mm/$\frac{1}{10}$″, Araldite, wood stain.

**Method.** The aim is to make your pieces of rock look like a modern sculpture. In the photograph opposite the large stone is 22 cm/9″ wide and the base is 13 × 11.5 × 4 cm/5 × $4\frac{1}{2}$ × $1\frac{1}{2}$″. With the hacksaw cut two lengths of iron or brass rod − one 5 cm/2″ piece for the large stone, and one 24 cm/$9\frac{1}{2}$″ piece for the smaller stone. In the base of each stone drill a hole 1 or 2 cm/$\frac{1}{2}$ or $\frac{3}{4}$″ deep. Hold the stone in a vice while you drill if you are using an electric drill, or between your knees if you have a hand one. Drill two holes 1 or 2 cm/$\frac{1}{2}$ or $\frac{3}{4}$″ deep in the wooden base, wherever you want to place the stones. Fix the rods in place with Araldite, and stain the base if you want to.

# Primitive jewellery

**Materials.** Pebbles (polished or natural), pieces of strong leather (buy scrap bags from leather dealers), leather or suede thonging, Araldite, Stanley knife or leather cutter, strong cardboard, leather punch, hammer, leather dye, tracing paper.

**Method.** Make a paper pattern for the leather cut-out, following figs 1, 2, 3 or 4 on page 24. Remember that each diagram shows only half the pattern, so when you place your tracing paper over the chosen pattern, fold the paper double first and lay the fold on the dotted line. Then you can cut your own pattern out double. Lay the pattern on the wrong side of the leather, and trace round the outline with a ball-point pen. Protect your working surface with a piece of thick cardboard, and cut out the leather with the sharp knife or cutter, taking care to make vertical cuts.

Using a leather punch or bradawl, make holes for the thonging. For necklace no. 3 a 14 mm/$\frac{5}{8}$" punch was hammered in to make the two large holes (not forgetting the cardboard underneath the leather). The resulting two small round pieces of leather were used as appliqué on necklace no. 1. The dog-collar at the bottom and necklace 4 have slits cut with the knife instead of holes.

If you don't like the colour of the leather you can use a leather dye to bring out the colour of your pebbles. Glue them in place with the Araldite and keep them pressed in position with a clothes peg or a heavy book, until the glue has set. Thread the thonging and finish it off with a knot — keep the design simple.

You can, of course, produce many variations on these ideas.

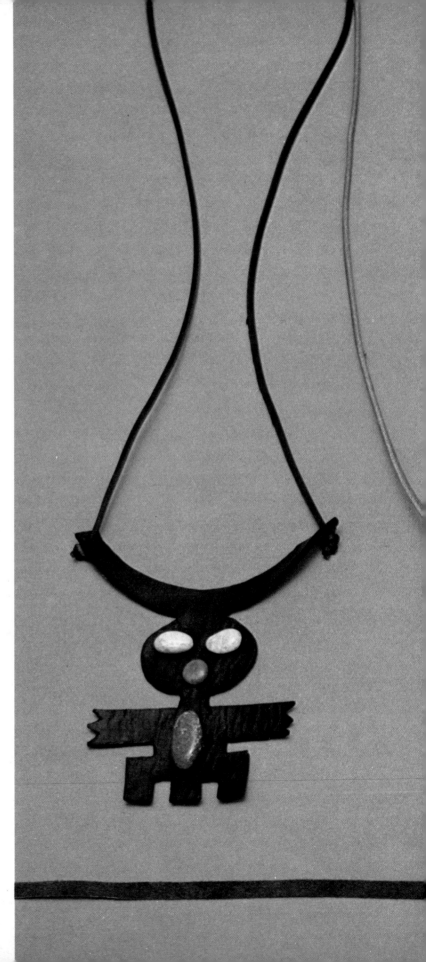

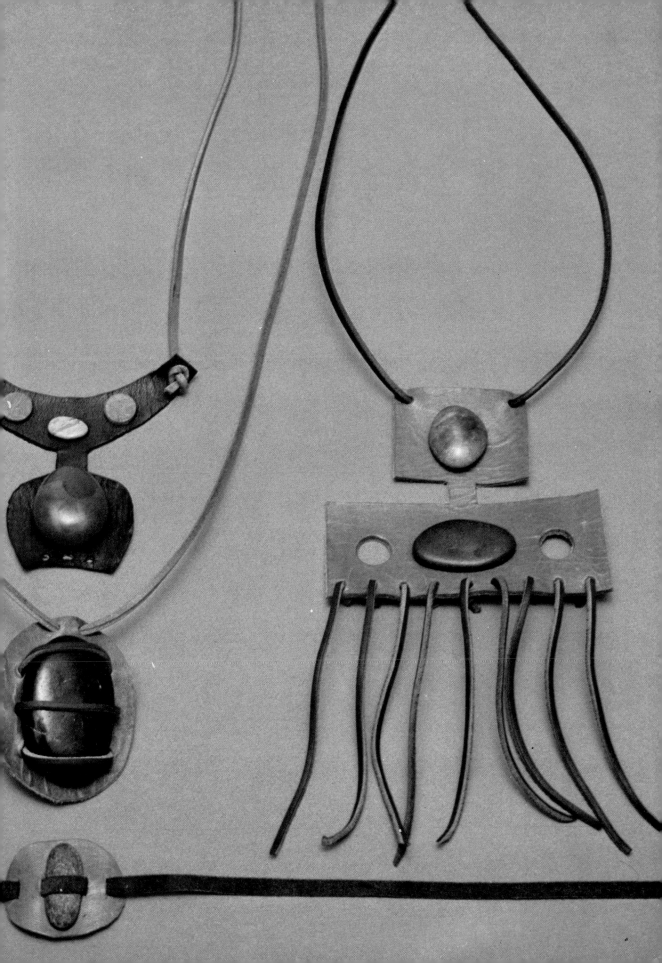

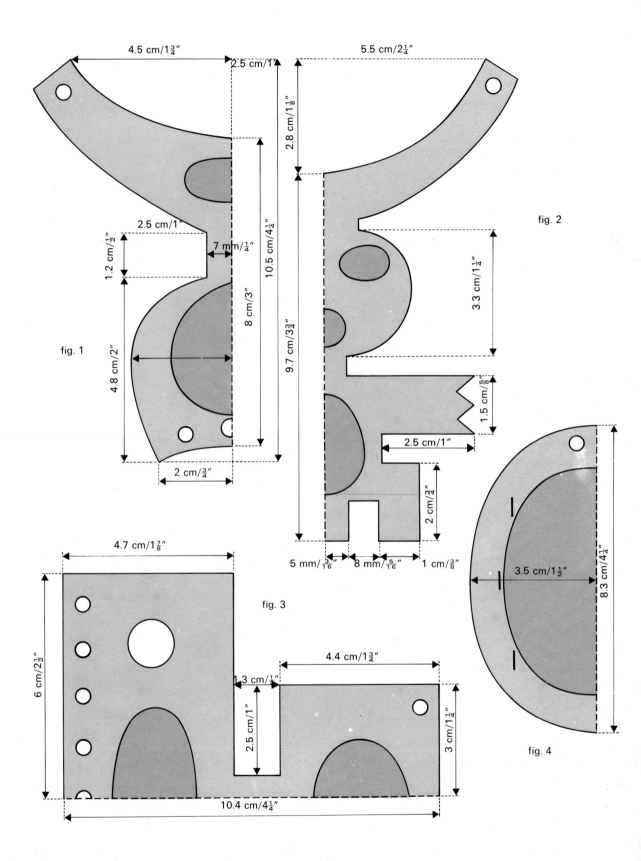

fig. 1

fig. 2

fig. 3

fig. 4

24

# Painted pebbles

**Materials.** Pebbles, white paper, soft pencil, black felt-tip pen, acrylic paint and brush.

Pebbles have inspired artists from prehistoric times. Let the shape of the stone start your imagination working.

**Method.** Draw round the pebble on white paper and make your design within the outline. Transfer it to the stone with a soft pencil, then go over the lines with a black felt-tip pen, and colour the areas within using two coats of acrylic paint.

# Witch doctor's mask

**Materials.** Flat piece of cork about 30 × 20 cm/12 × 8", various sizes of corks: two large flat ones 6.5 cm/2½" in diameter, two hollow ones 2.4 cm/1" in diameter, a dozen medium-sized ones, 20 small, and 25 wine-bottle size, quick-drying glue, 35 headless nails 2 cm/¾" long and 30, 4 cm/1½" long, hammer, acrylic paint in white, brown and red, paintbrush.

People don't often discover buried treasure but you can often transform driftwood, roots or bark into impressive modern art. The 'sculpture' on page 4 is a piece of trunk from a dead pear tree that had been eaten away by woodworm; treatment with insecticide was all that was needed, but usually you have to be more imaginative.

**Method.** Flat pieces of cork (perhaps part of an old bath mat) or bark or wood, together with bottle corks, can be used to make the face of this witch-doctor's mask. Sort out your corks, paint them with the acrylic colours and leave them to dry. To make eyes, fix the flat corks with a nail in the middle, and stick the hollow ones onto them with glue. The 2 cm/¾" headless nails, placed halfway along the side of each cork, will fix the ones for the nose to the base, but use glue as well to make sure they stick. Fix all the corks in the same way, using the larger nails for the biggest corks.

# Racing snails

**Materials.** Four or six snails for each player, metallic paint and solvent, pointed soft brushes, transfer numbers (e.g. Letraset) about 12 mm/$\frac{1}{2}$", or black paint, a few nails and a small ball of string, lettuce leaves.

**Method.** This is a snail race with a difference because the competitors look like racing cars. Paint their shells in bright colours, using metallic paint if possible to keep up the racing car image. Don't forget to clean the brushes in solvent afterwards.

While the shells are drying keep an eye on your snails, who might decide to take off without starter's orders. When the paint is dry, apply the transfer numbers, rubbing them on to the shell till the protective film comes off; alternatively you can paint numbers on in black acrylic paint.

The race is run over a straight course. Fix nails at the starting and finishing posts, and stretch string between to mark out each track. If you are racing on concrete, mark it out with coloured chalk. Each player chooses a colour and a track. If a snail crosses on to another track it is disqualified. Lettuce leaves at the finishing post will discourage dawdling.

When the race is over clean the competitors with solvent before returning them to their natural surroundings.

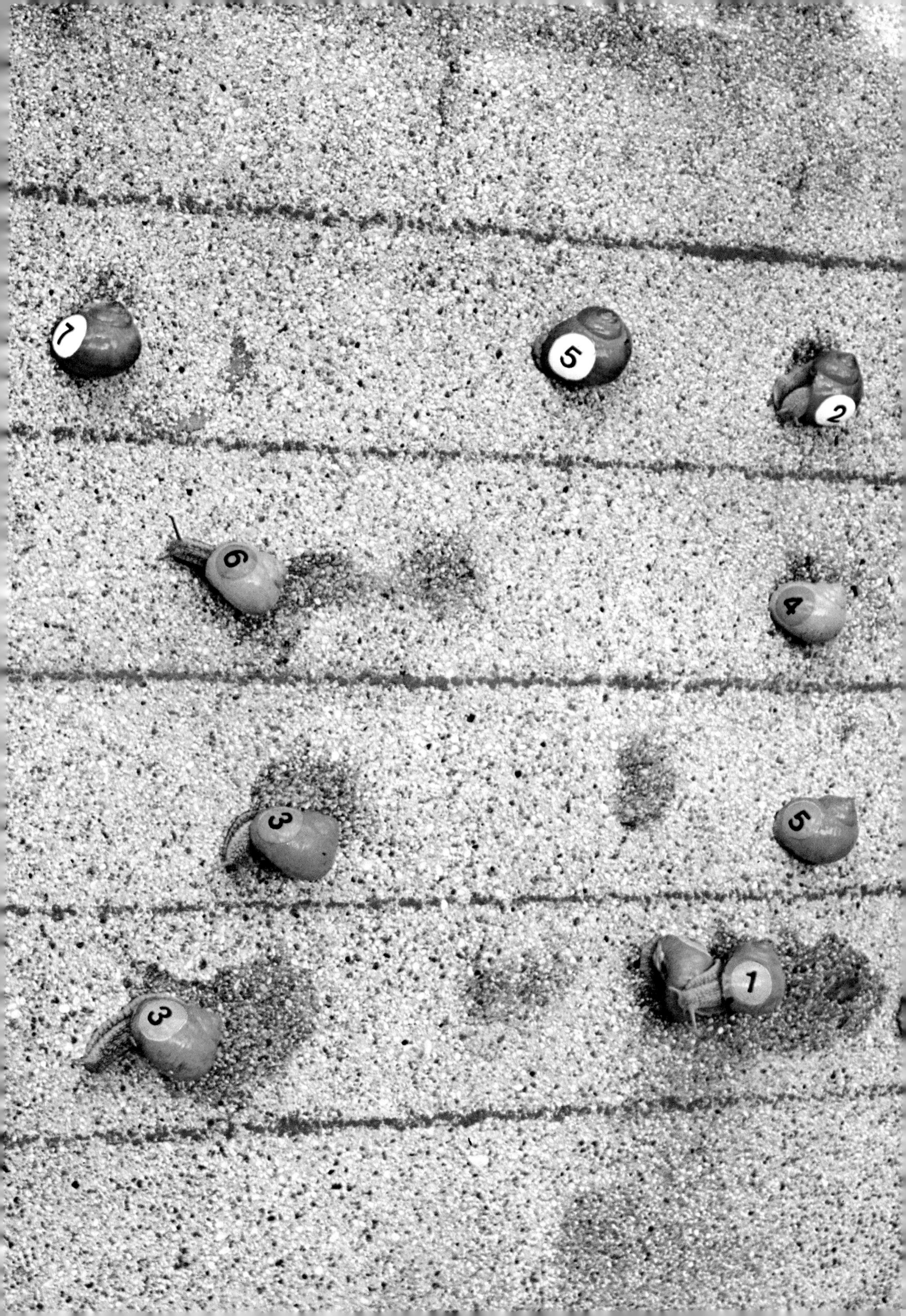

7
5
2
6
4
3
5
3
1

**Things to gather in summer**

Grasses, flowers, medicinal herbs, seaweeds, shells, maize-husks, straw.

**Lay in reserves for autumn and winter.** Seeds, flowers, reeds, straw, grasses, green leaves for drying, feathers, natural wool.

# Corn dolly

**Materials.** About 60 stalks of rye, wheat or barley at least 24 cm/10" long, strong thread (48 cm/20"), one or two clothes pegs, scissors.

Traditionally these corn dollies are hung in the house to bring good luck till the next harvest.

**Method.** Rye stalks are easiest to use, but wheat or barley will do. Choose about 60 stalks with well-formed ears which are not quite ripe (otherwise the seeds will fall as you work). If the straw is rather dry, soak it for a few minutes to make is less brittle.

Cut three or four stalks without ears about 16.5 cm/6½" long, and tie them in the middle with strong thread, making a small loop from which you can hang the finished dolly (fig. 1). The other stalks must be about 25 cm/10" long, including the ear. The first stalk goes on the left hand side of the loop (fig. 2). Hold it firmly in place with one finger and make sure the ear hangs vertically. The second stalk goes on the right of the loop (fig. 3), with the two ears level. Continue like this with the third, fourth and so on, so that the horizontal stalks on the left are on the wrong side of the dolly and the others on the right side. To prevent it unravelling, use clothes pegs to hold the last straws you have twisted in place, in other words hold the left side while you are working on the right, and vice versa.

When you have twisted the last two ears into place tuck their ends in as shown in fig. 4, and fasten them on the wrong side with thread. Cut the ends evenly with scissors, and the corn dolly is ready to hang on your bedroom wall.

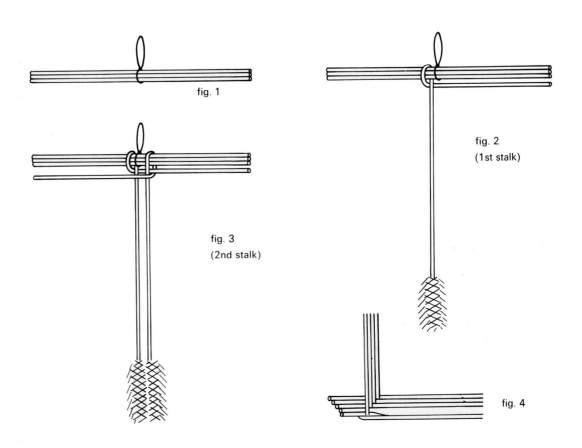

fig. 1

fig. 2
(1st stalk)

fig. 3
(2nd stalk)

fig. 4

# Dried flowers

There are a lot of plants, both wild and from the garden, which you can dry to use for decoration in the winter: St John's wort, wild mustard, everlasting flowers, golden rod, marguerites, heather, sea lavender, thrift, cornflowers, teasels, sea holly, thistles, reeds and the grass family, including oats, barley, millet and quaking grass. These grasses, like teasels and everlasting flowers, will dry on the plant, and you can wait till the end of the summer before cutting them. But choose the right moment for reeds because, if left too long, they will get fluffy.

Pick in dry weather when the plants are in full flower. Hang them, heads down, in a dry, *dark* place to keep the colours bright, especially the reds which fade easily. They will dry better if you make small bunches and separate the species.

Another method is to stretch wire netting horizontally over a box and poke the stalks through the holes so that the heads are supported by the mesh.

By the time the flowers are dry the stalks are sometimes broken; cut them off very close to the head, push brass wire into the centre of the flower, bend over the end in a hook and pull the wire gently so that it is fixed.

# Herbal remedies

Did you know that elderberries are good for coughs, that centaury stimulates the appetite, and hops are good for insomnia? Our great-grandmothers knew; herbal medicine has been practised from time immemorial and the healing properties of certain flowers, leaves and roots are generally recognized.

Gather them when it is dry and sunny, but not from dusty verges because you can't wash them. Don't take more of the plant than you need; if you are collecting leaves, take a few from several plants.

Divide them into species, spread them out on clean paper and dry them away from dust and light. Sunlight acts on the plants, drying up their essences.

When your plants are slightly papery put them into labelled jars. They are now ready to use in different forms of herb tea (infusions, decoctions or macerations). For an infusion, boiling water is poured on the plant; for a decoction it is put into cold water, brought to the boil and simmered for a few minutes; and for a maceration it is soaked in water overnight before being brought to the boil.

Here are a few of the many easily recognized types for summer picking.

| Plant | Part used | Treats | Prepared as |
|---|---|---|---|
| wormwood | leaves and flowers | indigestion | infusion |
| hawthorn | berries | high blood pressure | infusion |
| Aaron's rod | flowers | bronchial troubles | infusion |
| rest-harrow or cammock | root | liver, eczema | decoction |
| camomile | flowers | indigestion | infusion |
| lesser centaury | flowering plant | indigestion | infusion |
| chicory | flowering plant | clears the blood | infusion |
| marsh mallow | leaves, flowers and root | coughs, stomach troubles | infusion or maceration |
| hops | flowers | insomnia | infusion |
| mallow | leaves and flowers | bronchial and throat troubles | infusion |
| peppermint | leaves (before flowers appear) | indigestion | infusion |
| St John's wort | flowering plant | rheumatism | decoction |
| marjoram | flowering plant | coughs | infusion |
| wild pansy | flowering plant | clears the blood, diuretic | infusion |
| meadowsweet | flowers | rheumatism | infusion |
| wild thyme | flowering plant | bronchitis | infusion |
| elder | flowers | colds, flu, rheumatism | infusion |
| lime | flowers | acts as sedative | infusion |
| lady's finger | flowers | infected wounds | decoctions in compresses |

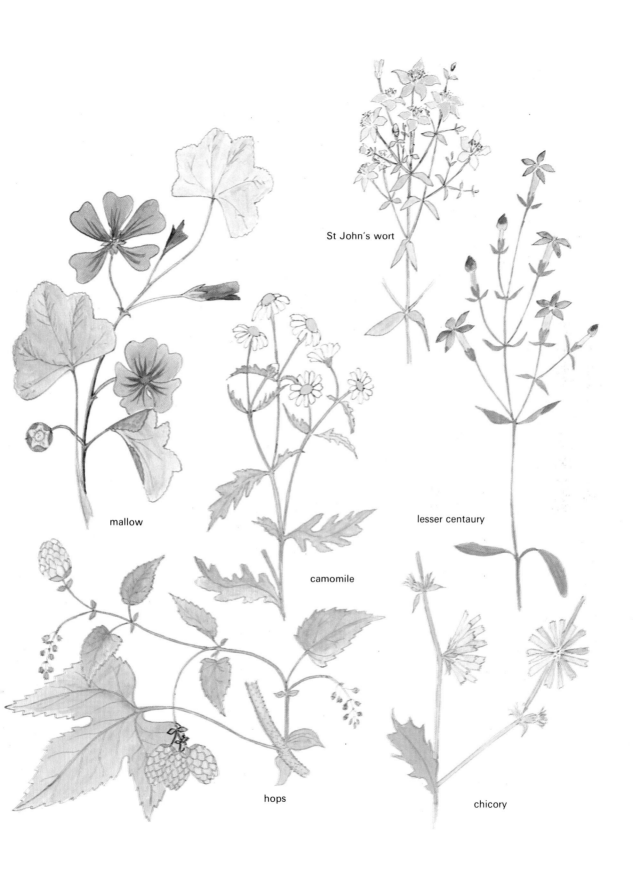

St John's wort

mallow

camomile

lesser centaury

hops

chicory

# Pressed seaweed and seaweed slides

**Materials.** Small bucket, tweezers, sheets of typing and blotting paper, knife, slow-drying glue.

There are some 20,000 species of seaweed — some are quite tiny, while others can be up to 30 m/100′ long. Collect them in rock pools when the tide is out. Cut the roots away from the rock with a knife, handling the seaweed carefully. Put it into a bucket full of seawater. At home lift the pieces of weed out one by one, slipping sheets of white paper under them. Spread them out with tweezers, lay a sheet of blotting paper over them, and leave to dry. Some seaweeds will stick to the paper by themselves; fix those that don't with a few drops of glue. They can be arranged like the pressed flowers (page 17), with a note of the species (identified with the help of books on seaweed), the place it came from, and the date.

You can also use seaweed to make slides, as described below.

**Materials.** Small pieces of seaweed, thin card, sheets of cellophane, penknife, ruler, scissors, tweezers, clear adhesive tape.

**Method.** Cut out for each slide a card rectangle 10 × 5 cm/4 × 2″. With a penknife score lightly along a line dividing the card exactly in two, and draw in windows, as in the diagram below. Cut out the windows very neatly, since the projector will magnify any rough edges. Turn the card over, smear a little glue round the openings and place a piece of cellophane 4 × 4 cm/1½ × 1½″ over each one. Fold the card along the scored centre line, with the cellophane inside, and your mounts are ready.

Open the mount and with the tweezers arrange little bits of different types of seaweed on one of the pieces of cellophane; fix them with tiny drops of slow-drying glue. Cover the frame of the mount lightly with glue, close it up and press both sides firmly together.

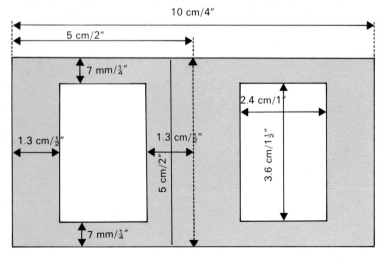

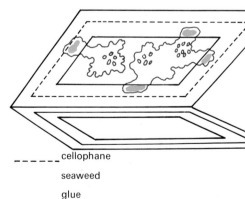

cellophane

seaweed

glue

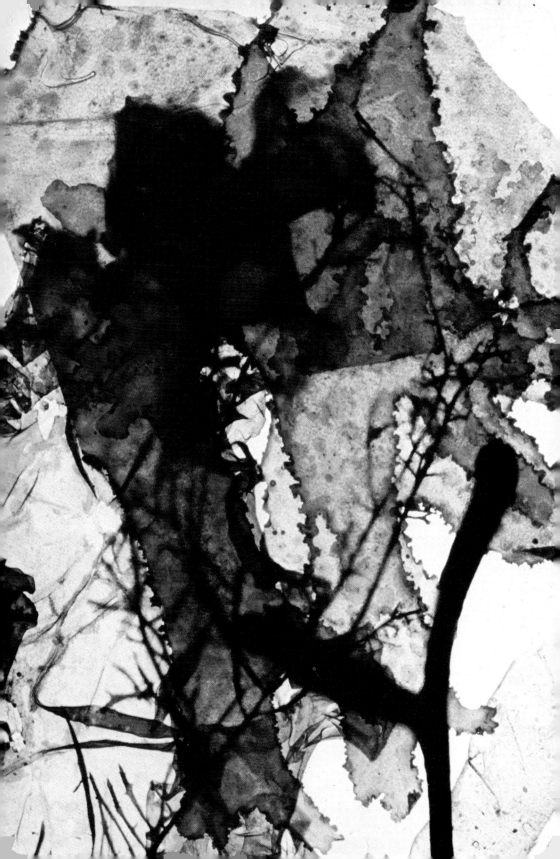

# Shells

**Materials.** Knife, bag you can sling over your shoulder, old saucepan, perforated spoon, bleach.

**Collecting.** The shells you find in dry sand on the beach are usually broken. To get perfect specimens you should go down to the rocks at low tide and examine the patches of seaweed and the rock pools. Be careful — don't get caught by the incoming tide, and wear shoes that won't slip on seaweed. If you climb rocks be sensible, never jump, and when you've got a foothold cling on with one hand too. Don't destroy marine life unnecessarily — leave small seaweeds and molluscs where they are, and always take an empty shell in preference to the live creature.

**Method.** Boil your catch for a few minutes. Take it out of the water immediately, using a perforated spoon, so that the shells don't lose their colour. Take the creatures out with a pin, and if some shells have weed on them slip them in bleach and scrub with a brush. Rubbing with an oily rag brings up their colour.

If you want to make a serious collection, number each shell with Indian ink and enter it in a notebook or card index with its scientific name, common name, where you found it, and the date.

door snails

netted dog whelk

turret shells

cockles

top shells

smooth venus

mussel

flat winkles

queen scallop

limpets

tellins

whelks

# Shell figures

**Materials.** Shells, modelling clay, quick-drying glue (e.g. Uhu), clear adhesive, black, orange and red ink, thinner and methylated spirits, fine brushes.

**Limpet Lady.** Pick about ten limpets which will go one on top of each other, with a big even one as the base. Spread glue round its point and set a second limpet on it. Continue with slightly smaller limpets (eight or ten), and finish off with one with a hole in the middle (you always find some like this). Glue the point of a whelk and fit it into the hole to form the upper part of the body. Leave to set. Then stick on the head — a flat winkle — and hold it in place for a few minutes with your fingers or adhesive. Two turret shells will make the arms. Stick them onto the whelk, and hold them in place until firm. For the hat use a scallop shell, trimmed perhaps with a yellow winkle as in the photograph opposite. The hair is made of tiny snails.

**Venus.** With a lump of modelling clay the size of a tangerine make a cone about 6 cm/2½" high as a basis for her skirt. Press damped venus shells into it, overlapping them. Stick a whelk into the top of the cone for the upper part of the body. If some of the shells fall off when the clay is dry, stick them back in place with slow-drying glue.

Make the head and arms in the same way as for the Limpet Lady. In the photograph above the arms are made from dog whelks, carnivorous shellfish which liquefy their prey with a kind of venom. The fore-arms are small door snails. As a final touch stick two tellins amongst the snails which make her hair. The ones decorating her skirt are painted pink with thinned red ink to pick up the colour of the tellins — but don't overdo the colour.

**Tortoise.** A limpet on four top shells, a small whelk for the head, and two dots of black ink for the eyes.

**Mouse.** A whelk, two tiny shells for the ears, a small tusk shell for the tail and dots of ink for eyes and nose.

**Penguin.** Moisten all the shells before using them. Stick a 4 cm/1½" whelk point-upwards in a piece of modelling clay the size of a nut. Put two small cockle shells underneath for feet. A yellow flat winkle fixed on with a small blob of modelling clay makes the head, and two mussel shells form the wings. Make sure the penguin stands firmly. If the clay has left a white deposit on the wings when it dries, touch them up with black ink. Finally, paint the feet orange.

# Golden cockerel

**Materials.** A packet of modelling clay, mussels, whelks and smaller shells, a cuttlefish bone, two toothpicks, glass tumbler, quick-drying glue, a few clothes pegs, aerosol gold paint.

**Method.** Mould a ball of modelling clay the size of an orange. Flatten it on one side and set it on the bottom of an upside-down tumbler. Make another ball of clay the size of a tangerine for the tail, and roll a third one into a cylinder for the neck and head. Fix these two onto the large ball with toothpicks (fig. 1). Moisten all the mussel shells and stick them into the clay, starting with the tail and overlapping them. Cover the whole body and then stick the cuttlefish bone into the head to make the beak (fig. 2). Make the crest as in the photograph — one mussel shell in front, two mussels stuck together with quick-drying glue for the middle one, and three stuck together for the back one. Push the crests into the head. Mould two balls of clay the size of walnuts for the feet, and into each stick three shells horizontally and two vertically, the latter enclosing a small roll of clay (fig. 3).

Leave to harden for two days. If any shells come unstuck glue them in place as described on page 41. Stick the whelks and snails on the head and neck with glue, holding them in place for 15 seconds. Stick together mussel shells for the tail, using clothes pegs to hold them together while the glue hardens.

Take the body off the tumbler and glue the legs onto it. To make the cock stand firmly stick an extra shell low on the tail, to touch the ground.

Spray the cock with gold paint, protecting anything in the vicinity with newspaper, and paint the eyes any colour you fancy.

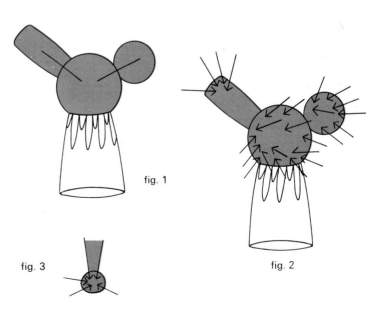

fig. 1

fig. 3

fig. 2

# Peasant dolls

**Materials.** Maize-husks, balls of cotton wool, strong thread, scissors, brass or copper wire (10 cm/4″ for each doll), the hairy part of the maize.

These typical central European dolls are easy to make, but they need a little patience. The maize-husks should be fresh and flexible. If they seem rather dry, soak them in warm water for a few minutes and then dry them between sheets of newspaper. Keep the brightest-coloured ones to make the dolls' clothes.

**Woman.** Wrap one of the balls of cotton wool in a whole husk at least 4 cm/$2\frac{1}{2}$″ wide, and twist the two ends of the husk to make the neck. Tie tightly.

To make arms, roll two or three husks, 10 cm/4″ long, lengthwise round a piece of wire (fig. 2) and tie 8 mm/$\frac{3}{8}$″ from the ends to make hands (fig. 3). Wrap each arm in a 8 cm/3″ square of husk (fig. 4). Tie, and turn the husk back over the arm to make a puffed sleeve. Tie another thread to hold the sleeve (fig. 5, overleaf).

Roll very tightly about ten leaves 10 cm/4″ long in the same way as for the arms, but without the wire. This forms the body. Tie it 2 cm/$\frac{3}{4}$″ from the end. Now slip the arms and body between the two long ends of husk hanging from the head, and tie the body at the waist (figs 6 and 7).

For the skirt, lift the arms, wrap several large husks round the body and tie them at the waist (fig. 8). Turn the husks down carefully and cut them off at skirt length. Make an apron, cap and so on if you like; before putting on the cap flatten the corners of the head. Make the hair from the hairy part of the maize.

**Man.** Make him in the same way as the woman, but make two rolls of husks for the body so that it has trousered legs.

**Child.** Use the same method, but make the doll much smaller.

The distaff, faggot and basket are fixed by a stitch or a drop of glue. Don't forget to paint in eyes on all the dolls.

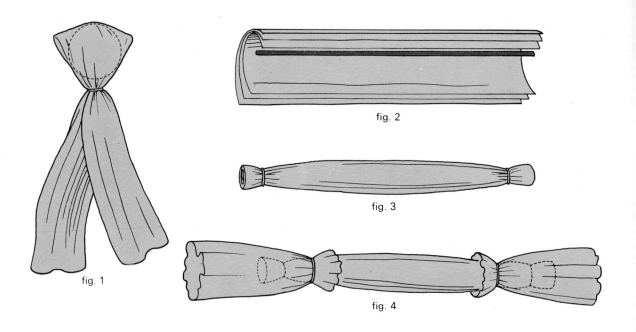

fig. 1

fig. 2

fig. 3

fig. 4

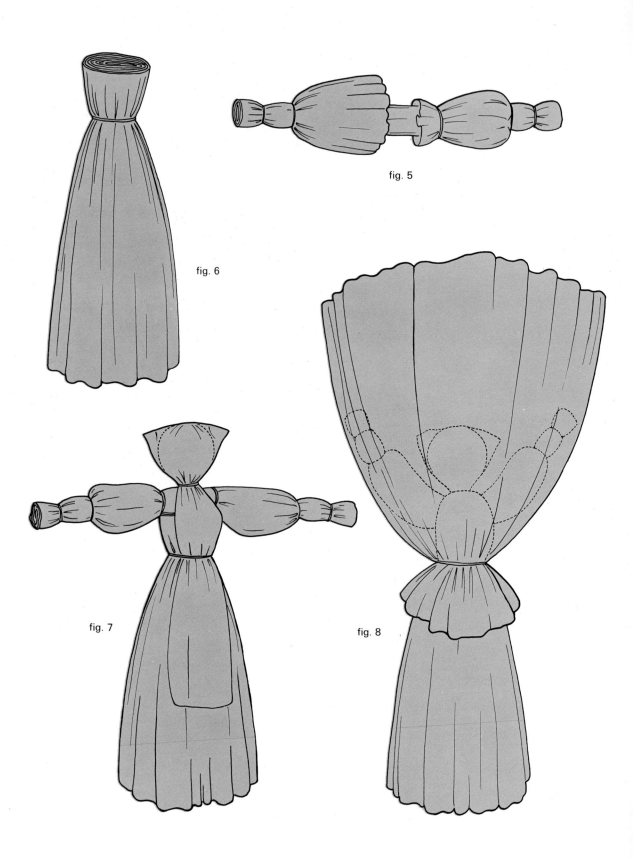

fig. 5

fig. 6

fig. 7

fig. 8

# Jackstraws

**Materials.** Straw, scissors, sewing thread, red and green ink, methylated spirit, gold or coloured paper, soft florist's wire.

**Method**

1. **Plain straws.** Cut 50 straws about 12 cm/5" long, choosing ones without joints. Colour 20 red or green with ink on a sheet of newspaper. Clean the brush with meths.

2. **Hook.** Stick a pin at an angle through the end of a straw 12 cm/5" long (fig. 1).

3. **Forks.** Use a 15 cm/6" straw for the handle. Thread a piece of wire through a 9 cm/3½" straw, bend it into a U-shape and fix it on to the handle about 3 cm/1⅛" from the end, looping a thread round and knotting it (fig. 2).

4. **Stars.** For each star you need 12 straws 8 cm/3" long. If the straw is very dry, soak it in warm water for a few minutes before using it. Make two bunches of six straws each, and tie each in the middle with thread. Separate the ends fanwise (fig. 3) and lay one bunch across the other. Tie them together, passing the thread between the straws to keep them separated (fig. 4). Cut the ends even with scissors and stick on a small round of gold or coloured paper to cover the thread. You need two or three stars to play the game.

**How to play.** This is an older version of the game also known as 'Spillikins', but it is played in the same way. The first player takes all the straws, plain and made-up, and drops them in a heap on the table from a height of about 50 cm/20". Using the hook, he extracts as many straws as he can without disturbing the rest of the pile. If he moves another straw he must give the hook to the next player, who does the same, and so on until all the straws have been removed. Then players add up their scores — plain straws count for one point, coloured two, forks five, and stars ten.

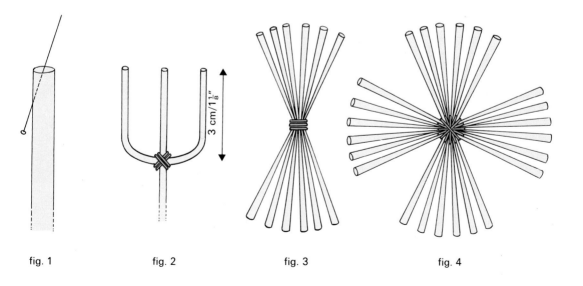

fig. 1    fig. 2    fig. 3    fig. 4

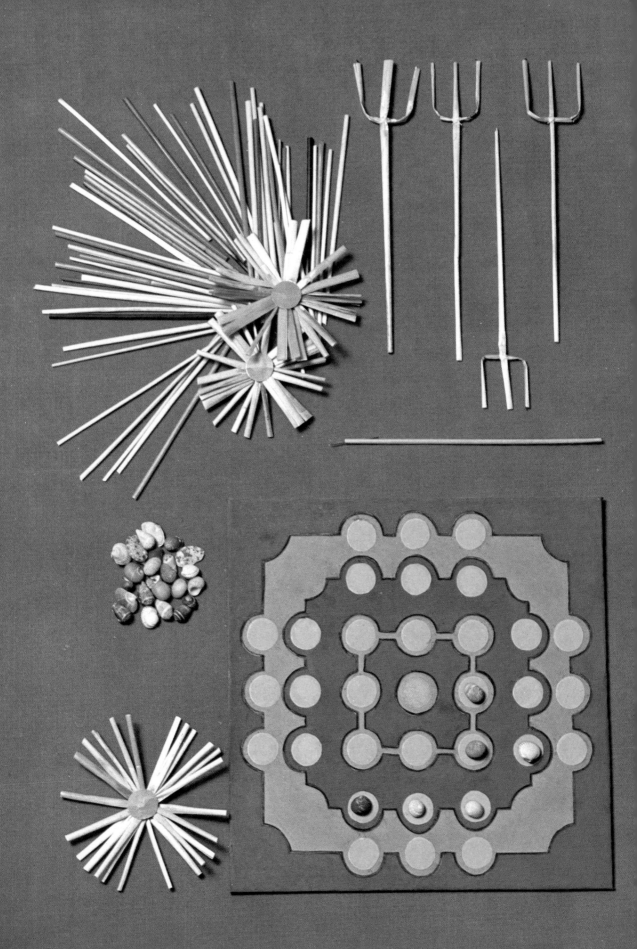

# Solitaire

**Materials.** Square of cardboard 22 × 22 cm/8½ × 8½", adhesive-backed paper in three colours: 25 × 25 cm/10 × 10", 25 × 10 cm/10 × 4", and 3 × 3 cm/1¼ × 1¼", baize or felt 21 × 21 cm/ 8½ × 8½", slow-drying paste, ruler, compasses, scissors, black felt-tip pen, acrylic gouache, brush, 31 small shells.

A Frenchman imprisoned for years in the Bastille invented this game to pass the time.

**Method.** Lift the 25 cm/10" square of adhesive-backed paper from its backing and lay it on the cardboard with a 1.5 cm/½" overlap all round. Smooth it by hand to remove any air bubbles, and fold it over, cutting the corners as in fig. 1.

Paste the back of the baize or felt and lay it on the back of the cardboard, leaving a 1.5 cm/½" margin all round. This stops the board slipping. Smooth out air bubbles. Copy the outline pattern in fig. 2 onto the board, using a felt-tip pen. Paint the green area in fig. 2 with acrylic gouache, choosing your own colour to contrast with the background. With compasses draw 32 circles of 75 mm/$\frac{5}{16}$" radius on the 25 × 10 cm/10 × 4" sheet of adhesive-backed paper, and a single circle on the 3 cm/ 1¼" square piece. Cut out circles, remove the backing and stick in the positions shown by dotted lines in fig. 2, putting the odd one in the centre.

**How to play.** This, as the name suggests, is a game for one player. Place a shell on all but two circles, one of these being the centre one. You can move shells, one at a time, in any direction except diagonally. One shell jumps over its neighbour into a vacant circle, and the neighbour is removed. To win you must get all the shells off the board except one, and that one should end up in the centre circle. Try with only 28 shells the first time — it's easier!

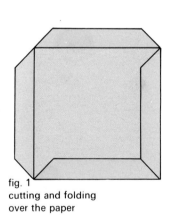

fig. 1
cutting and folding
over the paper

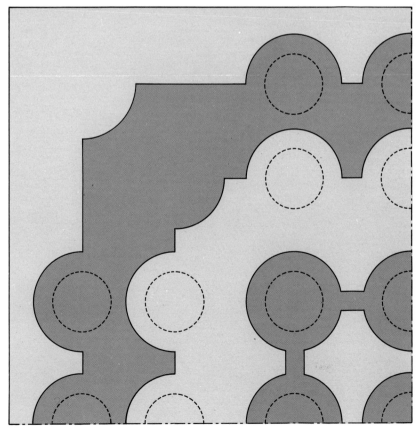

fig. 2
a quarter of the solitaire
board, actual size

**Things to gather in autumn**

Leaves, flowers, reeds, elder branches, gourds, horse chestnuts, lichen, acorns, sycamore keys, pine, cedar and other cones, plane seeds, natural wool, feathers, maize-husks.

autumn

# Autumn leaves

Autumn is the best time of the year for collectors. Some late flowers are especially easy to dry, for instance small chrysanthemums, heather and thistles (see page 34).

    Leaves can be used decoratively, too. Stop them shrivelling by putting them in a solution of 1 part glycerine to 2 parts water. Crush the ends of the stems and stand them in the mixture for 10–15 days. If you run melted candle wax over the ends it will help to stop the solution evaporating.

# Woodland Bird

**Materials.** Mixed dried leaves, drawing paper, rubber cement, thick cardboard and glass the same size as the drawing paper, framing materials (frame clips, ring for hanging up):

**Method.** The leaves must be dried flat, between newspaper, under a pile of books. Lay them on drawing paper in the shape of the bird, then stick each one on separately with rubber cement; it dries slowly, so you can have second thoughts and move them around without damaging them.

Put cardboard, picture and glass together and secure them with clips. Then fix a ring to the back.

# Greeting cards

**Materials.** Dried leaves, piece of velvet about 15 cm/6″ square, old toothbrush, plain cards, white or coloured, gouache, brush, rubber cement.

**Method.** Use last year's leaves if possible, or ones which have been well dried under a pile of books in a warm place. Lay the leaf on the velvet and tap it gently with the toothbrush. The dried fleshy part will disintegrate, leaving only the lacy skeleton. Stick it with rubber cement onto plain cards, and add stylized leaves in gouache to make distinctive greeting cards.

# Decorated bottles and jars

**Materials.** Seeds (bean or lupins), needles, gimlet, pliers, coloured inks and solvent, brush, ball of embroidery cotton or thin string, quick-drying glue, bottle and jam-pot.

**Method.** Clean the seeds, and leave them to dry on newspaper in a dark, dry place. Before they get too hard, pierce them with a fine needle and enlarge the hole with a coarser needle or fine gimlet. Paint the seeds with coloured ink, thinned with solvent. When dry, turn the seeds over to paint the other side. You can thread them to make necklaces and bracelets, or to decorate various objects.

**Decorating a bottle with macramé.** Thread an even number of beans on 20 cm/8" thread. Push the threaded needle right through the bean, using pliers if necessary. Between each pair of beans knot a thread, as in fig. 1. Doubled, it should be three times the height of the carafe. Tie the string of beans with its 12 double threads round the neck of the bottle. Then make two rows of macramé, like this:

First row: take the threads four by four, and knot them as in figs 2, 3, 4 and 5. Fig. 6 shows the result.

Second row: use the same knot, but this time take two threads from the right with two from the left-hand set (fig. 7).

Now thread a lupin seed on the two centre threads of each set of four, then make a macramé knot, as above, with the four threads (fig. 8). Then thread a seed on each of the two outer threads of each set of four (fig. 9). Continue knotting until the bottle is covered. Make a second row of beans round the base, and tie all the threads from the macramé onto the thread running through the beans. Cut the ends about 2 cm/1" from the knot and glue them evenly under the base.

You can cover the jam-pot in the same way.

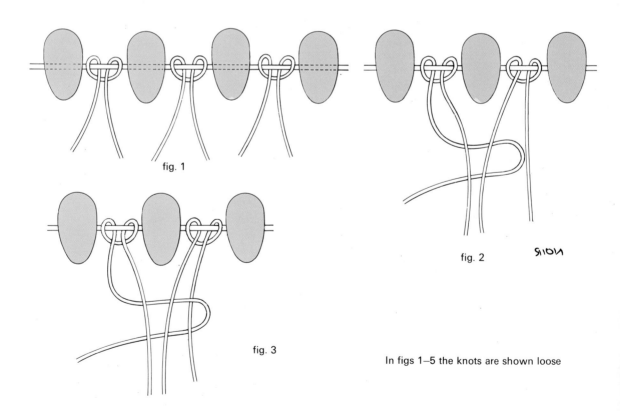

fig. 1

fig. 2

fig. 3

In figs 1—5 the knots are shown loose

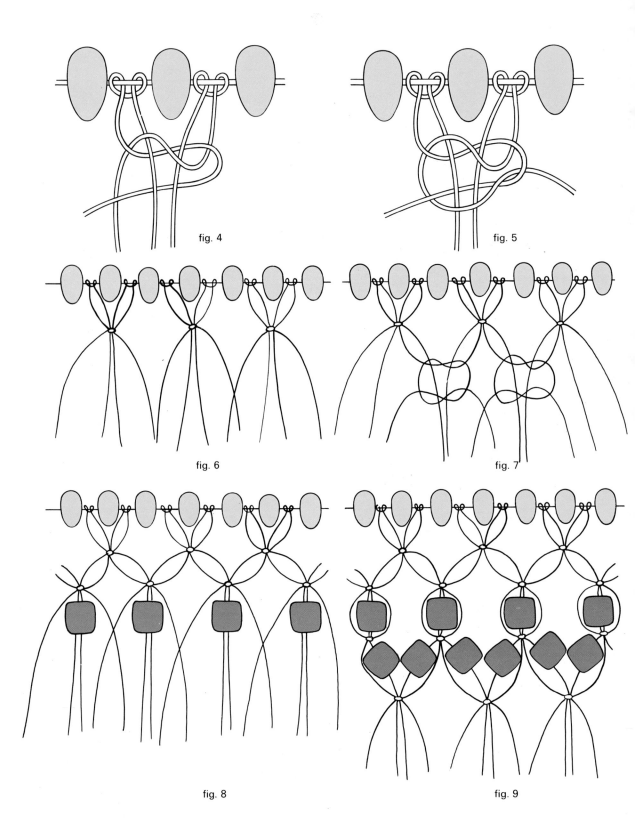

fig. 4

fig. 5

fig. 6

fig. 7

fig. 8

fig. 9

# Seed collage

**Materials.** Seeds, either collected or bought from a grocer or seed merchant (e.g. maize, sunflower, melon, millet, marrow, poppy heads, lentils, soya beans, sorghum, lupin seeds or haricot beans), sheet of grey card 55 × 40 cm/22 × 16", tracing paper, same size as the card, two tubes of quick-drying glue.

**Method.** It's not a very good idea to paint the seeds because their natural colours go so well together; but if you've got a few left over from the previous job — the red lupin seeds for example — you can use them carefully, to set off the subtle colours of the rest on their grey background.

Trace one of the designs below, and then transfer it to the card. Separate the seeds into cups or small jars. Start in the middle of each flower and apply the glue straight from the tube onto the middle circle on the card. Keep inside the outline. Stick large seeds on individually, but pour the small ones — carefully. Continue gluing the card and applying the seeds, always working outwards from the centre of each flower. Make the stalks in the same way, and finish off with the large outlining seeds.

You can stick gold or silver braid all round the edge, if you like, to make a frame, and fix a picture hanger on the back.

A: peppercorns, lupin seeds, sorghum, maize, poppy heads.
B: maize, water-melon seeds, sunflower seeds, sorghum, tops of poppy heads (use a knife to separate them from the poppy heads).
C: lupin seeds, sunflower seeds, lentils, millet, soya beans, marrow seeds.
D: millet, lupin seeds, peppercorns, maize, millet, water-melon seeds, white sunflower seeds.
E: peppercorns, maize, sorghum, soya beans, poppy heads.

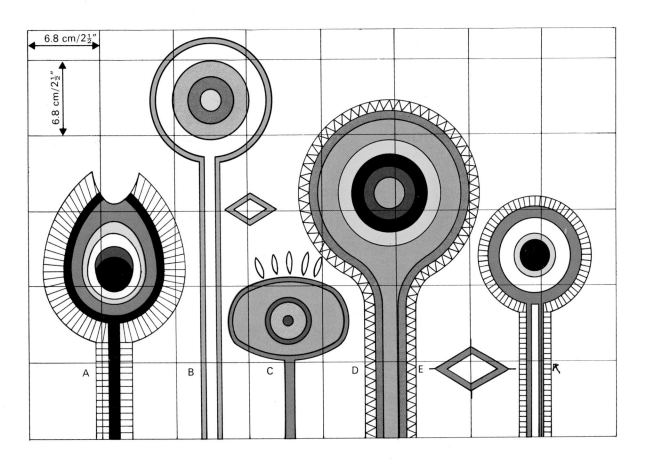

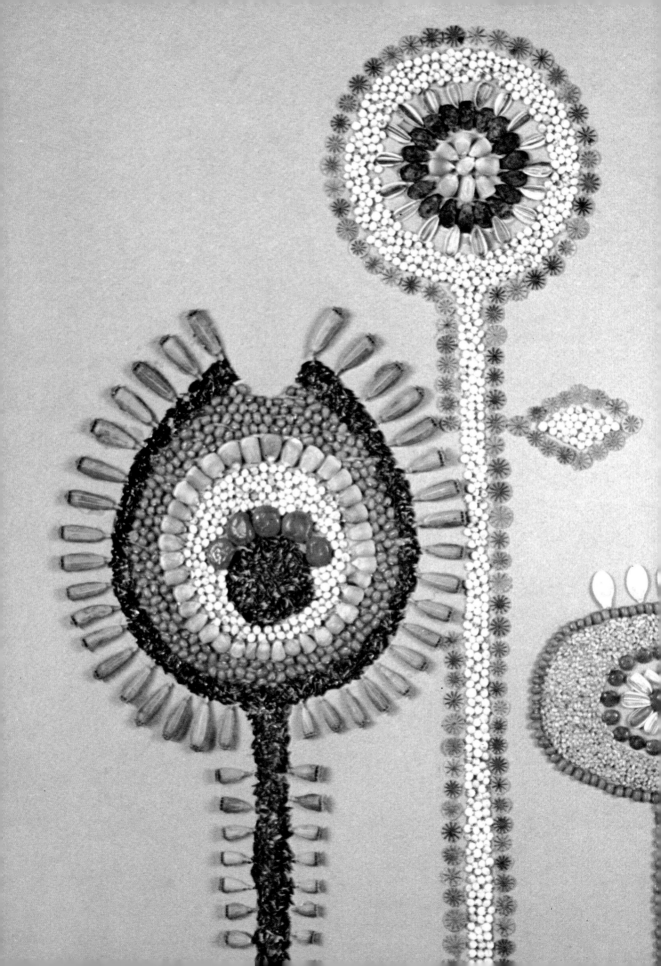

# Victorian posy

**Materials.** Dried flowers (everlasting flowers, honesty, grasses), black felt or velvet 54 × 40 cm/ 21 × 16", 6 mm/$\frac{1}{4}$" plywood, 46 × 32 cm/18 × 12$\frac{1}{2}$", piece of 6 mm/$\frac{1}{4}$" thick polystyrene 40 × 60 cm/18 × 24", stapler, or hammer and upholstery tacks, pins, 50 cm/20" ribbon, slow-drying glue. For the frame: 3 mm/$\frac{1}{8}$" plywood – two pieces 46 × 5 cm/18 × 2", and two pieces 32.6 × 5 cm/ 12$\frac{3}{4}$ × 2", black felt or velvet the size of the four pieces of ply, slow-drying glue, 24 headless nails, thin glass 46.6 × 32.6 cm/18$\frac{1}{4}$ × 12$\frac{3}{4}$", roll of coloured framing tape (passe-partout), picture hanger ring, varnish.

**To make the mount.** Cut two pieces of polystyrene, one the same size as the plywood (46 × 32 cm/ 18 × 12$\frac{1}{2}$"), the other 42 × 28 cm/16$\frac{1}{2}$ × 11". Lay on a table: (1) the big piece of velvet, soft side down; (2) the big piece of polystyrene, so that there is a margin of cloth about 4 cm/1$\frac{1}{2}$" all round; (3) the smaller piece of polystyrene, carefully centred; (4) the piece of plywood exactly over the big piece of polystyrene. Pressing firmly on the plywood, bring the edges of the cloth over it, pulling them tight, and staple or nail them all round, starting in the middle of each side. Mitre the corners to reduce bulk (figs 1 and 2). Turn it over and it's ready for the posy.

**Posy.** (If you are going to frame it make the frame first – see below.) Cut the stalks of the everlasting flowers and honesty close to the head, but leave the grass stalks about 8–10 cm/3–4" long. Keep a few stalks longer than this. Fix the everlasting flowers by pushing a pin at an angle through the middle of each flower into the cloth and polystyrene. Pin the long stalks in place, hiding the pins under the flowers and the ribbon bow. Arrange the grasses all around, sliding their stalks under the flowers. Handle honesty with care, fixing each head separately with a dab of glue which will also help to anchor the grasses. Now all you need is a pretty bow of ribbon, held in place with a few carefully concealed pins.

**To make the frame.** Cover the four pieces of plywood with slow-drying glue, and stick on the felt or velvet smoothly. Now fit them, cloth side inwards, onto the mount and fix with small headless nails (fig. 3). Fix the picture hanger on the back. Arrange your posy (see above), varnish all the exterior parts, and when dry fix the glass in place with passe-partout picture framing tape, mitred at the corners (fig. 4).

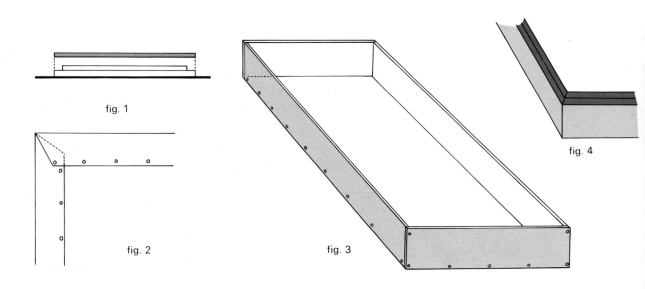

fig. 1

fig. 2

fig. 3

fig. 4

# Make your own music

**Materials.** Bamboo, reeds and elder branches, knife, strong thread, coloured embroidery silk (three skeins), cigarette papers, small rubber bands, small gourds, teaspoon, acrylic paint in pink, orange and black, brush, poker, handful of wheat or barley grains, two 20 cm/8" pieces of 2 cm/$\frac{3}{4}$" dowelling, wood rasp, glasspaper, quick-drying glue, varnish.

The simplest of all materials can be made into musical instruments, from a reed-pipe to a full orchestra. A kazoo, bamboo flute, Pan's pipes and Caribbean maracas will be enough to start with.

**Kazoo** (fig. 1). Cut a piece of elder branch about 15 mm/$\frac{5}{8}$" in diameter and 15–18 cm/6–7" long. Cut a hole, as shown, 4 cm/$1\frac{1}{2}$" from one end, then remove the pith from the branch by pushing a pencil or stick through it. Cover the ends of the tube with cigarette papers held on by rubber bands.

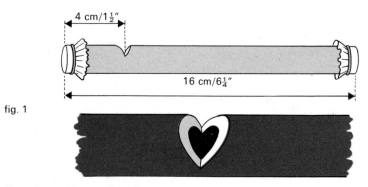

fig. 1

**Bamboo flute** (fig. 2). Cut a piece of bamboo 25 cm/10" long into two pieces, one 18 cm/7" long and the other 7 cm/3" long. Cut a sliver of wood off B, and make five holes about 6 mm/$\frac{1}{4}$" in diameter with a red hot poker. (Get an adult to help, just in case you burn yourself.) Shave down the end of piece A away from the joint so that 15 mm/$\frac{5}{8}$" of it fits inside B. Remove a sliver from A, then cut a second sliver into the hollow of the bamboo without detaching it (see fig. 2). Push A into B; put the flute in your mouth as far as the red line, and blow.

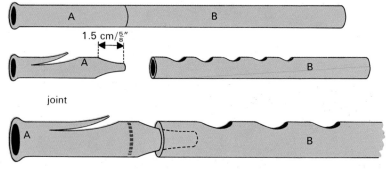

fig. 2

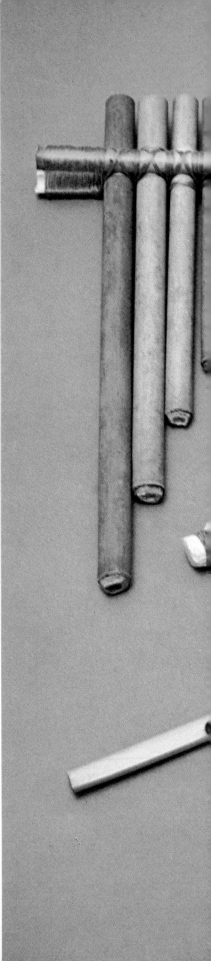

**Pan's pipes.** Cut pieces of bamboo of different lengths, sawing them off at the joint so that they are closed at that end and open at the other (fig. 7). Shorten them at the open ends to get a series of different notes — hold the bamboo vertically and blow across the end, not into it. Shorter, thinner pipes give high notes, and longer, fatter ones low notes. With a good ear and knife at the ready you can make up a scale. Lay your pipes in order of size between two pieces of split bamboo, making sure the open ends are exactly level. Fix the first pipe with strong thread (figs 1–5), then the others (figs 6–7), ending up with a tassel.

The measurements in the drawings are only intended as a guide — the actual measurements will vary according to the thickness of your bamboo.

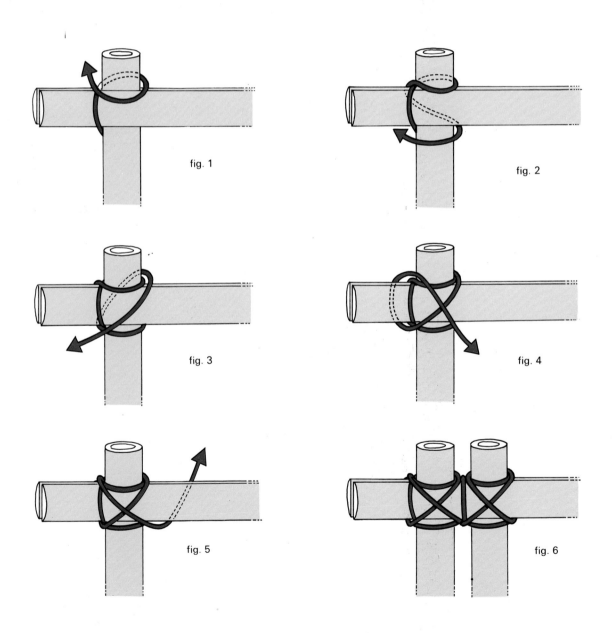

fig. 1

fig. 2

fig. 3

fig. 4

fig. 5

fig. 6

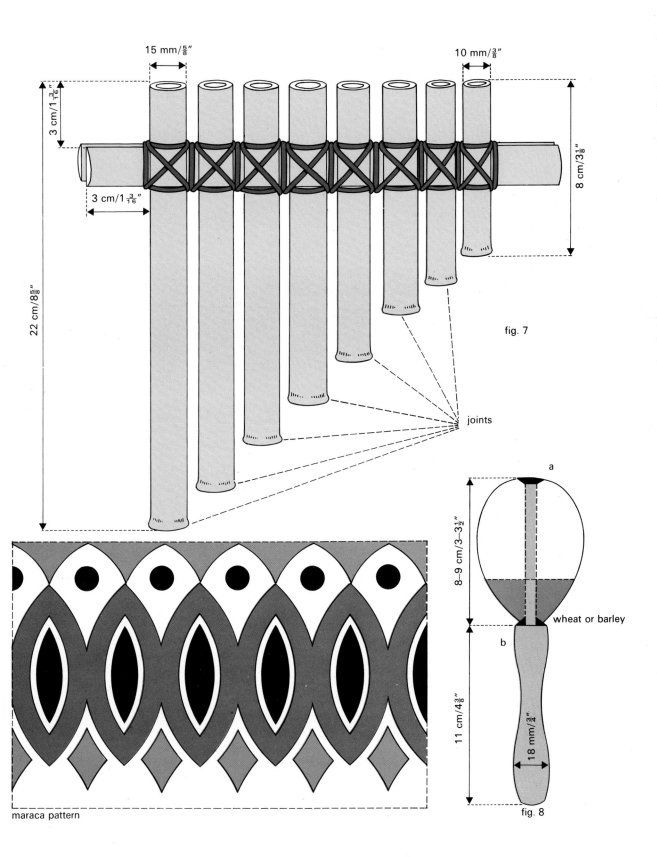

15 mm/⅝″

10 mm/⅜″

3 cm/1 3/16″

8 cm/3⅛″

3 cm/1 3/16″

22 cm/8⅝″

fig. 7

joints

a

8–9 cm/3–3½″

wheat or barley

b

11 cm/4¾″

18 mm/¾″

fig. 8

maraca pattern

**Maracas.** Choose two well-shaped gourds and leave them for several days in a dry, well-aired place. Cut them off at the stalk, making a round hole with a narrow-bladed knife. Scrape out the inside with a teaspoon handle, then leave them to dry, hole downwards. After three or four days the remaining pulp will loosen; remove it with a spoon handle. After another four or five days they will be ready for use.

With the knife, shape two handles out of dowelling and stick them into the gourds. The tip of the handle should fit neatly into the curved end (see (a) on fig. 8, page 65), and the base must fit the hole (b). Shape the handles with a rasp, smooth them with glasspaper and varnish the exposed part. Fill the maracas a quarter full with wheat or barley grains. Fix the handles, gluing at a and b, with quick-drying glue (fig. 8).

Draw the pattern shown — or any other pattern that you like onto the maracas, and paint it in with acrylic paint.

Gourds dried in this way can also be used for making puppets (page 88).

# Calabash flask

Take a large bottle-shaped gourd and prepare it as above. When dry and hard it will be very good for keeping drinks cool. Fit a cork into the opening. The macramé cord is made from 4.5 m/5 yards of fine string. If you are learning to drink Spanish-style, pouring drinks into your mouth from a height, practise with water first.

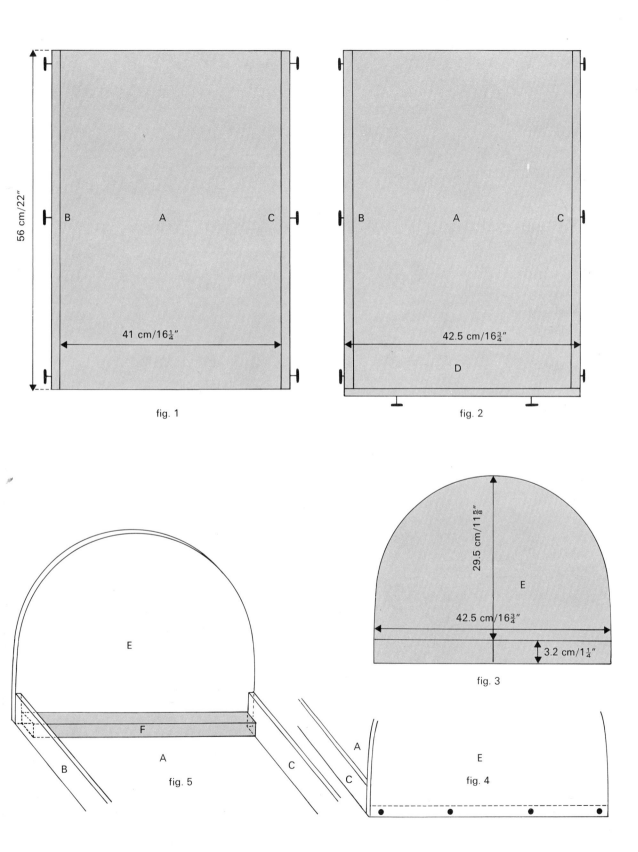

56 cm/22"

B    A    C

41 cm/16¼"

fig. 1

B    A    C

42.5 cm/16¾"

D

fig. 2

29.5 cm/11⅝"

E

42.5 cm/16¾"

3.2 cm/1¼"

fig. 3

E

F

A

B

fig. 5

A

C

C

A

E

fig. 4

67

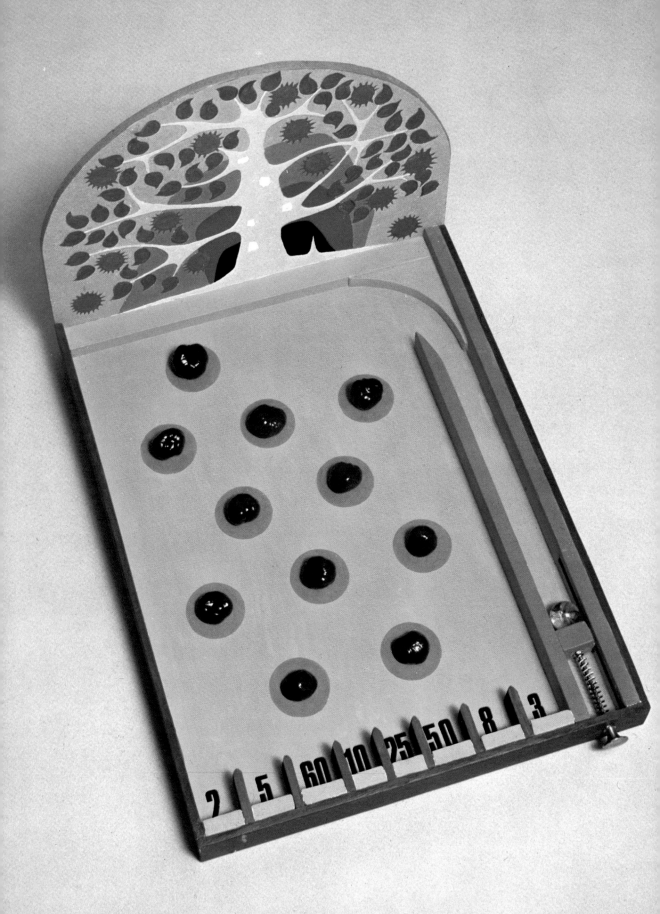

# Flipper board

**Materials.** Sheet of 16 mm/$\frac{5}{8}$" ply 41 × 56 cm/16$\frac{1}{4}$ × 22", two strips 0.7 × 4.5 × 56 cm/$\frac{1}{4}$ × 1$\frac{3}{4}$ × 22" (B and C), one strip 0.7 × 4.5 × 42.5 cm/$\frac{1}{4}$ × 1$\frac{3}{4}$ × 16$\frac{3}{4}$" (D), one strip 1.6 × 2.5 × 41 cm/$\frac{5}{8}$ × 1 × 16$\frac{1}{4}$" (F), sheet of 1 cm/$\frac{3}{8}$" plywood or chipboard 32.7 × 42.5 cm/14 × 16$\frac{3}{4}$" (E), two strips 1.5 × 2.8 cm/$\frac{9}{16}$ × 1$\frac{1}{8}$" one 53.5 cm/21" long (G), the other 44 cm/17$\frac{1}{2}$" long (H) (they can be bought ready grooved on one side), one 3 cm/1$\frac{1}{4}$" cube (I), seven pieces 0.7 × 2.8 × 5 cm/$\frac{1}{4}$ × 1 × 2", one strip 1.6 × 2.8 × 30 cm/$\frac{5}{8}$ × 1$\frac{1}{8}$ × 12" to cut blocks for the numbered scoring sections. Other materials – 4 mm/$\frac{3}{16}$" threaded rod 7.5 cm/3" long, spring 6.5 cm/2$\frac{1}{2}$" long, small drawer knob, two rubber feet, 24 2.5 cm/1" wood screws, glass marble or ball-bearing, small conkers. Tools – saw, gouge, screwdriver, gimlet, drill, paint brushes, glasspaper, wood glue. Paint – white primer for acrylic paint, acrylic gouache in yellow, orange, red, turquoise, ultramarine, white and black.

**Method.** (If you've never done any carpentry you may need some friendly help.)

1. **The board.** Fix B and C to the base A with 2.5 cm/1" screws (fig. 1 on page 67). Then screw down D. Remember to drill holes for the screws beforehand. Use fig. 3 to mark out on board E the outline shown. Saw round it and then smooth the edge with glasspaper. Fix the board E to the base A with four screws (fig. 4). Glue F to A and E between sides B and C (fig. 5).

2. **Working parts.** If G and H are not ready grooved, use the gouge to cut a channel in each 10–15 cm/4–6" long (fig. 6). Saw the end of H to a curve, and smooth it with glasspaper (fig. 9). Cut cube I as shown in fig. 7, so that it slides easily in the grooves of G and H. Glue G to base A and side C. Bore a hole in I and fix the threaded rod into it. Fit I into the groove of G and bore a hole in end D for a rod to pass through. Slip the spring on to the rod, pass the end of the rod through the hole in D, and fix the knob on to it. Pulling on the knob tightens the spring and pulls back the hammer, I; releasing it lets the hammer shoot back into place.

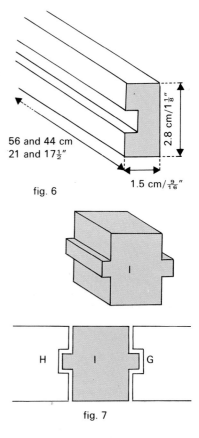

56 and 44 cm
21 and 17$\frac{1}{2}$"

2.8 cm/1$\frac{1}{8}$"

1.5 cm/$\frac{9}{16}$"

fig. 6

H    I    G

fig. 7

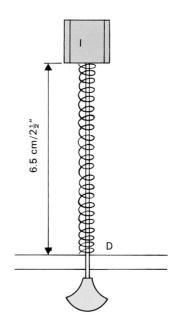

6.5 cm/2$\frac{1}{2}$"

I

D

fig. 8

Place H parallel to G, so that the hammer I moves freely along the grooves. Mark and glue in place. Then drill from under the base and screw G and H firmly in place (fig. 9).

Using wood left from making E, cut the corner piece J. Sand it, and glue it down in the corner of F and G (figs 9 and 10). It will help to direct the marble when in play.

3. **Numbered scoring bays.** Cut each of the seven 2.8 × 5 cm/ 1 × 2″ blocks as in fig. 11. Glue them to the base and to D (fig. 12). To hold them firm, cut blocks to glue between them (fig. 13). Fix two rubber feet under the baseboard at the end marked E (fig. 14).

4. **Painting.** Cover the whole surface with white primer, using a flat brush, so that the wood will not soak up the coloured acrylic paint. When dry, draw the pattern shown on pages 72–3 onto the board E (enlarge the pattern to fit the board), and paint in the colours. Paint the baseboard and put in the numbers (figs 15 and 16). Glue small conkers on the board (fig. 16).

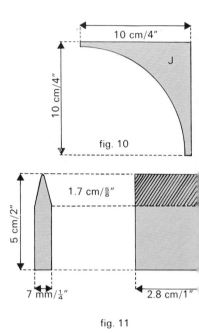

fig. 10

fig. 11

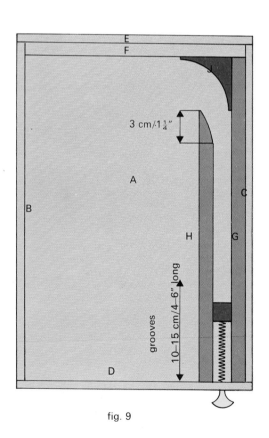

fig. 9

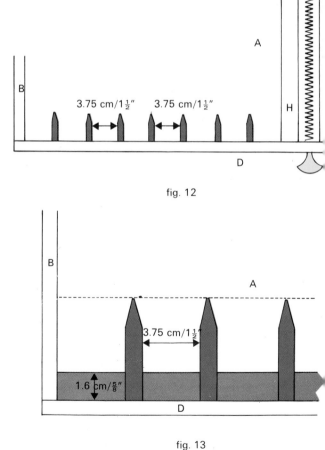

fig. 12

fig. 13

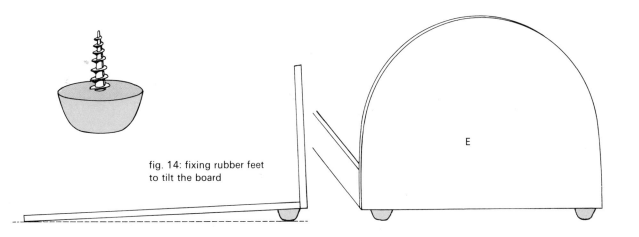

fig. 14: fixing rubber feet
to tilt the board

E

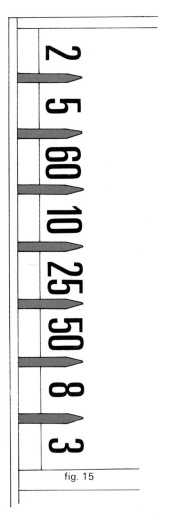

fig. 15

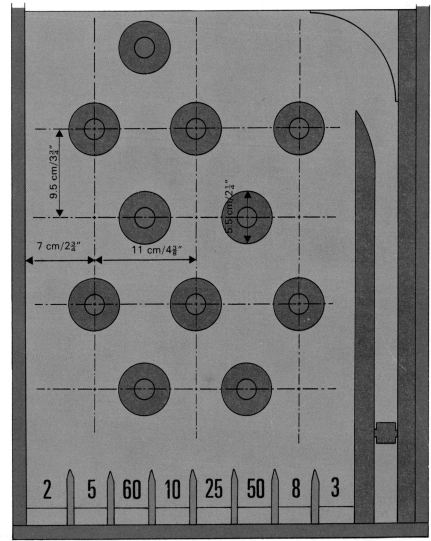

9.5 cm/3¾"

5.5 cm/2¼"

7 cm/2¾"

11 cm/4⅜"

2   5   60   10   25   50   8   3

fig. 16

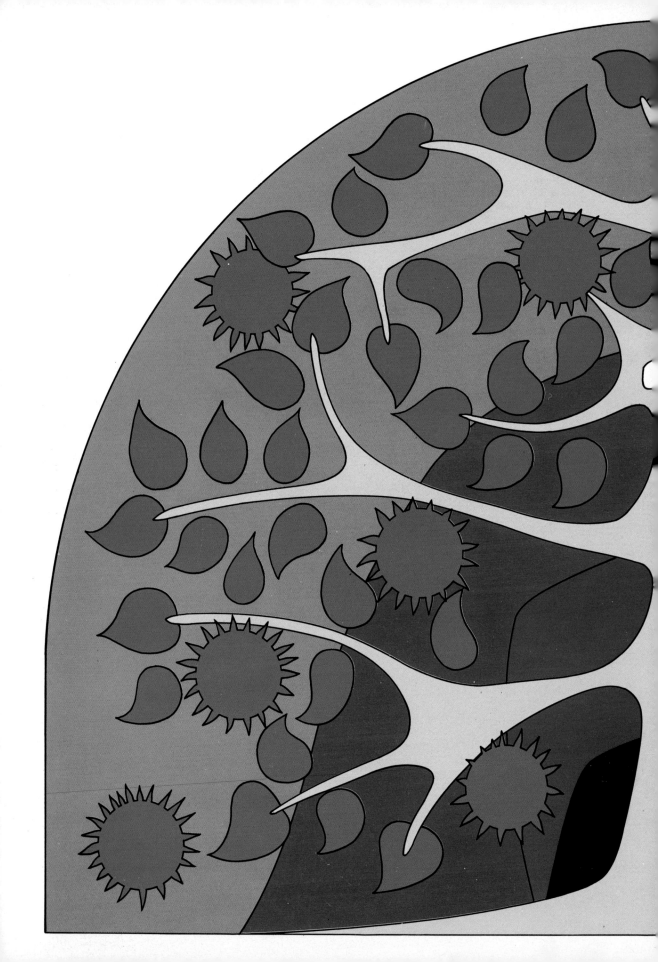

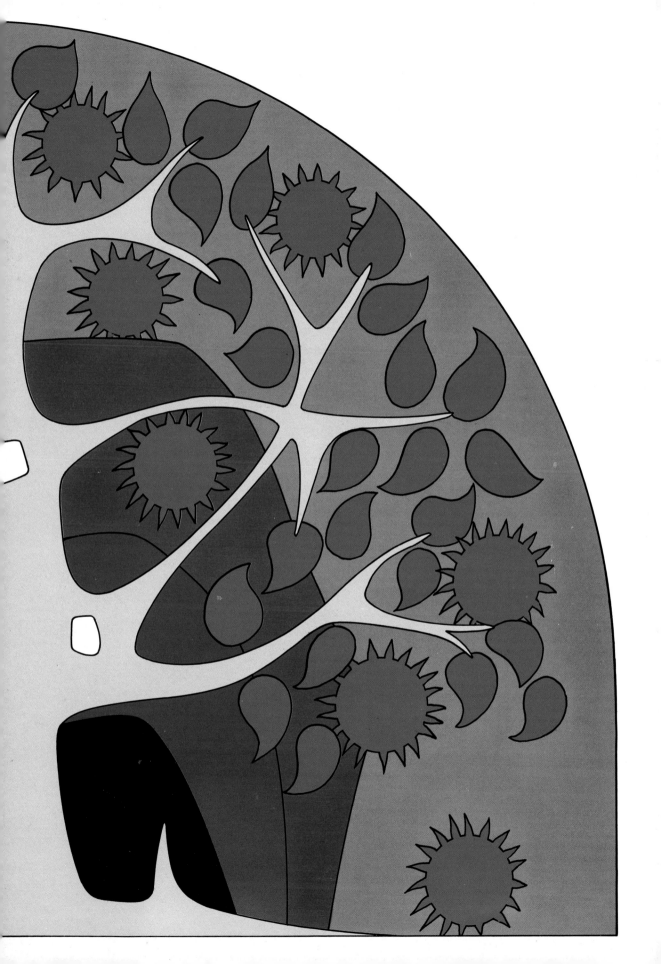

**Things to gather in winter**

Lichen, seeds, cones. Use the things you have in store from earlier in the year.

winter

# Fantastic insects

**Materials.** Dried leaves and flowers, feathers, seeds, twigs, pine cones and needles, plane and maple seeds etc., quick-drying glue (e.g. Uhu), slow-drying glue, knife, piece of cloth, toothpicks, vice, drill, saw.

**Method.** Add your own fantastic varieties to the 700,000 species of insect that exist in nature. The bits and pieces of flowers and seeds you collected in summer and autumn will provide materials and ideas. Begin by sticking together thorax and abdomen, the heaviest parts, with quick-drying adhesive. Hold them in place for a few minutes and then leave them on a piece of cloth on a flat surface so that they won't move. Glue on the more fragile elements last of all: first head, then wings, jaws, antennae, feet. Stick the most delicate materials (such as honesty pods for wings) with lighter adhesive. You can strengthen joints by spearing the different parts on toothpicks, but boring a hole is a delicate job. A small vice and drill will help. To use scales from a cone, saw it in half and detach the individual scales with a penknife.

## Suggestions

1. Cypress cone, acorn, pine needles and scales, cape gooseberry.
2. Walnut shell, plane seed, pine scales, acorn, cherry stalks, toothpicks.
3. Pine scales, maple keys, melon seeds, ilex acorns, cherry stalks, toothpicks, cloves.
4. Avocado stone, leaves, gorse flowers, small thistles, sunflower seeds, pine needles.
5. Poppy head, maple keys, leaves, dried daffodil petals, sunflower seeds, cherry stalks, toothpick.
6. Chestnut husk, cypress cone, shell, ilex acorns, cherry stalks, melon seeds, dried beans.
7. Acorns (large and small), honesty, cherry stalks.
8. Pine cone, poppy and catchfly heads, sunflower seeds, grasses, autumn leaves, anemone petals.
9. Cape gooseberry, small shell, catchfly head, honesty, cherry stalks, dried beans.

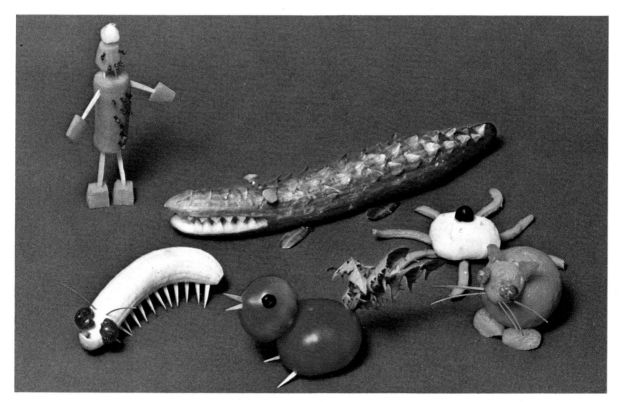

# Edible zoo

These animals are decorative, amusing and you can eat them too. You will find the materials and tools you need in the kitchen. It is best to choose vegetables and fruit which can be eaten raw.

## Hors d'oeuvres

**Cucumber alligator.** Cut off a strip of skin for the mouth, and cut the teeth with a pointed knife. Cut some peel off the 'under-belly' and make feet from it. The juice will help them to stay in place. Raise little scale-like triangles on the back with the point of a knife. Make the eyes from two circles of orange peel fixed with bits of toothpick.

**Red bird.** Use two tomatoes fixed together with a toothpick, and dandelion leaves for the tail. Almonds make the beak, and two more toothpicks the claws. The eyes are pieces of black olive or currants.

## Main dishes

**Squid.** Stick eight french beans into a boiled potato, with an olive in the middle.

**Robot.** Cut a big carrot, raw or cooked, into pieces, and fix it together with toothpicks. Place a small white onion on top. Use cloves for the eyes, mouth and knobs on his switchboard.

## Desserts

**Centipede.** Cut four or five toothpicks into small pieces and stick them into a banana. Two cherry stalks or pine-needles are the feelers, two glacé cherries make the eyes, and a piece of candied peel the mouth.

**Cat.** Use an orange and a dried apricot. The ears and paws are cut out of the apricot, with currants or raisins for eyes, and pine-needles or cherry stalks for whiskers.

# Sheep's wool bag

**Materials.** A very simple loom, odd lengths of wool, cotton or linen, natural sheep's wool gathered in summer, three leather thongs.

Grazing sheep leave wool on hedges and bushes. Gather it and remove all dirt by washing in warm, soapy water. Tease out each handful into a thick irregular yarn – you will have differing lengths and shades of colour.

**Weaving.** Set up the warp of the loom with linen or strong cotton thread. You need a warp 20 cm/8" wide, on which to weave a 75 cm/30" length (fig. 1). When the warp is ready, thread the shuttle with linen, wool or cotton. In the photograph, the pocket part of the bag is woven in coarse bouclé linen. Beat up the weft threads firmly with the reed to make the cloth strong. Weave a 44 cm/18" length, and then start weaving in the natural wool. Pass it through the warp with your fingers, blending in the different tones. When you have woven 16 cm/6" of this, finish off by passing a double linen thread 60 cm/24" long through the warp (fig. 2). Cut off the warp threads, leaving 15 cm/6" for a fringe, and knot as shown in fig. 3.

Sew up the bag with a 22 cm/9" seam at each side and attach a strap plaited from three leather thongs.

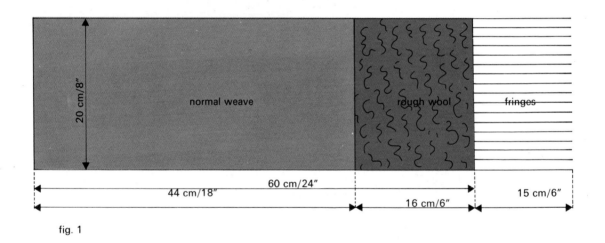

fig. 1

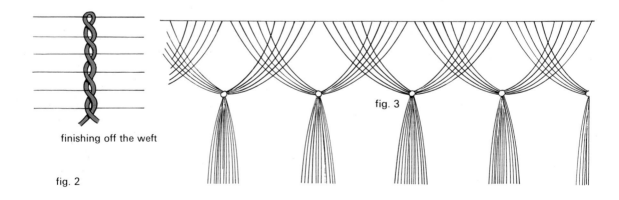

finishing off the weft

fig. 2

fig. 3

# Leaf tapestry

**Materials.** Simple loom, reel of strong twist, pressed leaves (maize, maple, elm, oak), wheat or rye straw.

**Weaving.** Set up a warp with twist, to the size you want, spacing it twice as wide as normal (see fig. 1). Meanwhile soak the leaves and straw in warm water, taking them out as you need them. Start weaving normally with twist, beating it up with the reed, and complete 1 cm/$\frac{1}{2}$". Now add a maize-husk, for example, and leave it flat. From now on the weft will not be perpendicular to the warp, but will follow the contours of the leaves. Push them up gently with your fingers. Go on putting in a variety of leaves and straws, and hold them in place by weaving a few rows of twist in between. At the end of the tapestry choose straight-sided leaves to give a horizontal finish, then put in a few rows of twist and beat up the weft with the reed. Tie the warp as shown in fig. 2 on page 80, and cut the threads to take it off the loom. Dry it under a pile of books to stop it curling up. After a few days the tapestry will be ready to be hung on your wall, or in front of a lamp or window there the light will bring out the warm tints and delicate patterns of the leaves.

How to set up the warp on a loom

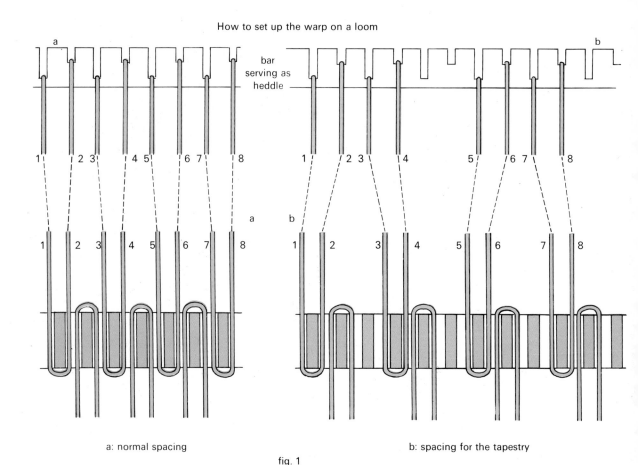

a: normal spacing

b: spacing for the tapestry

fig. 1

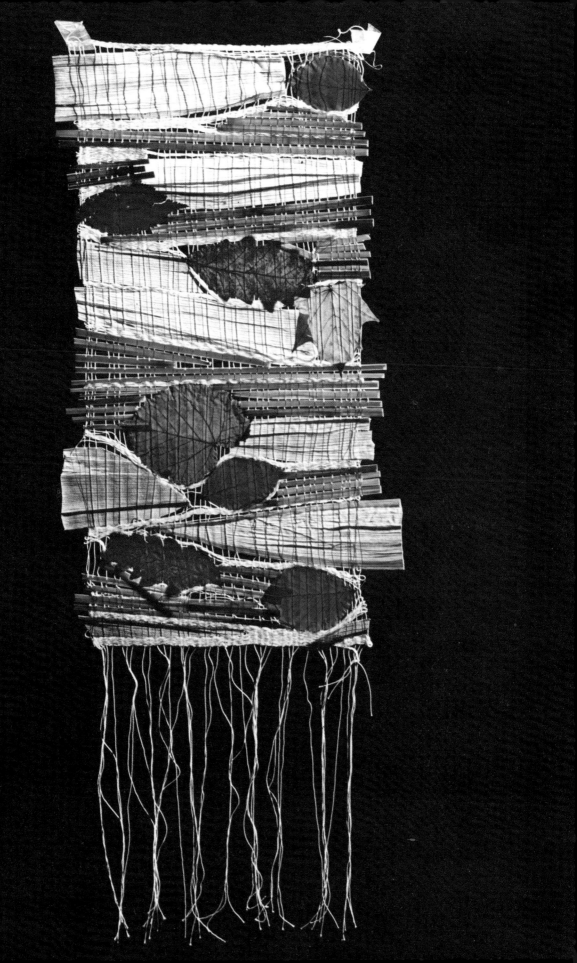

# MARCH 19..

| Monday | Tuesday | Wednesday | Thursday | Friday | Saturday | Sunday |
|--------|---------|-----------|----------|--------|----------|--------|
| 1 | 2 | 3 | 4 | 5 | 6 | 7 |
| 8 | 9 | 10 | 11 | 12 | 13 | 14 |
| 15 | 16 | 17 | 18 | 19 | 20 | 21 |
| 22 | 23 | 24 | 25 | 26 | 27 | 28 |
| 29 | 30 | 31 | | | | |

# Calendar

**Materials.** Twelve sheets of drawing paper 32 × 24 cm/13 × 10", Letraset figures and letters, Indian ink or a fine felt-tip, flexible (rubber-based) glue, leaves, seeds, feathers, shells.

**Method.** Make a calendar for the new year with twelve simple pictures. There is no need to frame them, because they won't get worn out in a month. You are sure to think of something for each month from the materials you have collected. Work out your patterns with the materials to hand, and stick them with a flexible adhesive.

Draw a frame for the month with Indian ink. Put Letraset sheet over your drawing paper in the exact position for the letter you need. Rub over it with a ballpoint and carefully lift the sheet off. If necessary, touch up with Indian ink.

The photographs here show for March peacock feathers, pressed leaves, melon seeds, ferns, grains of maize and millet; and for May pressed spring leaves, dried autumn leaves and heather, shells.

MAY 19..

# Festive candles

**Materials.** Candle wax, cotton wicks, cake of paraffin wax, knitting needle or ruler, empty tin, moulds (see below), punch, bowl and saucepan, brush, dried leaves and flowers, oranges, grapefruit, tangerines, undamaged nutshells, such as walnut halves, cooking oil, wax crayons.

**Perfumed oil lamp.** Cut a tangerine across the middle. Take out the edible fruit and the pith, but take care to leave the peel whole and the little centre stalk attached to it. Soak the inside of the peel and stalk with cooking oil; when you light the stalk, as if it were a candle wick, it should burn slowly giving out a pleasant perfume.

**Oranges, grapefruit and nuts.** Cut the fruit across the middle and remove the pulp, as above. The nutshells can be used as they are. Melt candle wax (a mixture of beeswax, paraffin and stearin, melting at 60°C/140°F) in a tin placed in a saucepan of water over heat (or a double saucepan, if you have one). *Never* try to melt wax in a saucepan directly over heat. The wax will burn and may catch fire. Add grated wax crayons to give colour, and stir the mixture with a spatula or old spoon.

Cut a 10 cm/4" wick for each half fruit (shorter for nuts). Curl 2 cm/¾" of the wick (again, less for nuts) into the bottom of the fruit or nutshell, pour a little wax onto it and let it harden; then pour in molten wax, holding the wick vertical, until the peel or nutshell is full. Cut the wick, leaving 2 cm/¾" above the wax. The nut candles are light, and can float in a water-filled dish.

**Large decorated candles.** Plastic bottles with the neck cut off make the best moulds. Make a small hole in the bottom with a hot skewer or knitting needle, pass a wick through and knot it underneath (fig. 1). Pull it up and tie it round a knitting needle or ruler resting on top of the mould (fig. 2). Heat the wax as before in a double saucepan. If you want to decorate the candles with leaves, etc., they will look more effective if the wax is left uncoloured. Put the mould in a bowl of cold water to speed up cooling. As wax hardens it shrinks; add a little more wax later to fill the hollow.

When the candle is cold, cut off the knot underneath, plunge the mould quickly into hot water, pull on the wick, and the candle should slip out of its mould. Cut the wick to 2 cm/$\frac{3}{4}$".

To decorate the candles, melt some paraffin wax in a double saucepan. Lay the candle on its side (fig. 3), spread leaves on it and brush a thin layer of wax over them. When this part is firm, roll the candle over and decorate the next part, and so on.

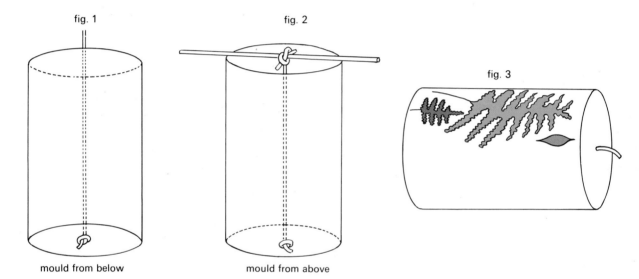

fig. 1

fig. 2

fig. 3

mould from below

mould from above

# Puppets

**Materials.** Five small gourds, five pieces of 18 mm/$\frac{5}{8}$" dowelling 35 cm/14" long, two corks, penknife, wood glue, slow-drying glue, adhesive tape, acrylic gouache, two skeins of wool or some sheep's wool, half a sheet of stiff paper, five pieces of cloth 50 × 70 cm/20 × 28" in bright colours including a blue, felt — white (20 × 5 cm/8 × 2"), black (32 × 72 cm/13 × 29"), brown (30 × 20 cm/12 × 8"), pink (10 × 15 cm/4 × 6"), beige (10 × 60 cm/4 × 24"), cotton wool, 1 m/1 yard fine string; two pieces of silk for scarves 22 × 22 cm/9 × 9".

**Making the puppets.** You will have prepared your gourds in autumn (see page 66). Now cut dowelling handles as for the maracas, then stand them in bottles so that you can work on them. Cut cork noses with a penknife and stick on heads with wood glue, holding them in place with adhesive tape till dry. Cut ears from stiff paper (fig. 1). Bend along the dotted line and stick on with slow-drying glue.

Paint head and ears with a uniform coat of gouache, pink or reddish-brown. When dry, paint on eyes, mouth and red cheeks. Hair and moustaches are made either from sheep's wool or from teased-out knitting wool stuck on in little tufts with slow-drying glue.

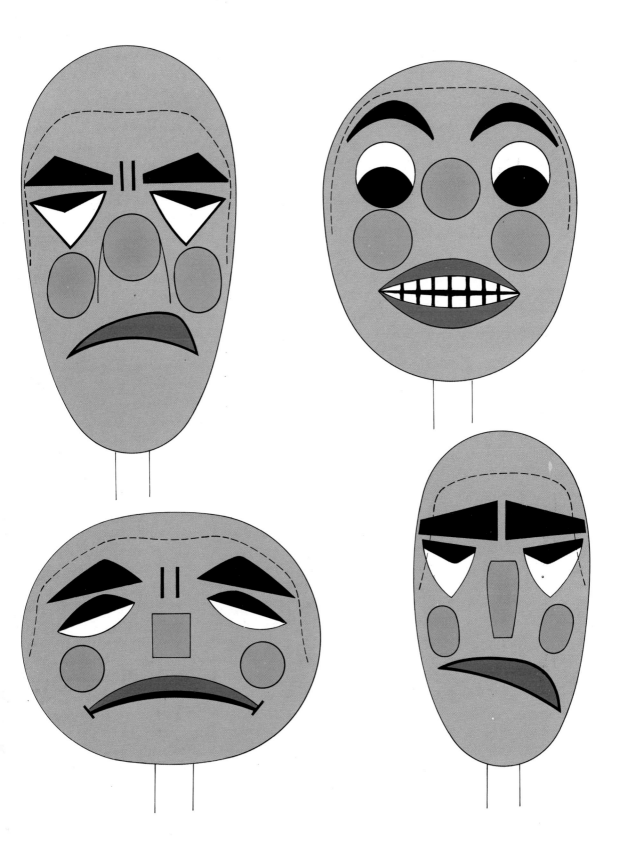

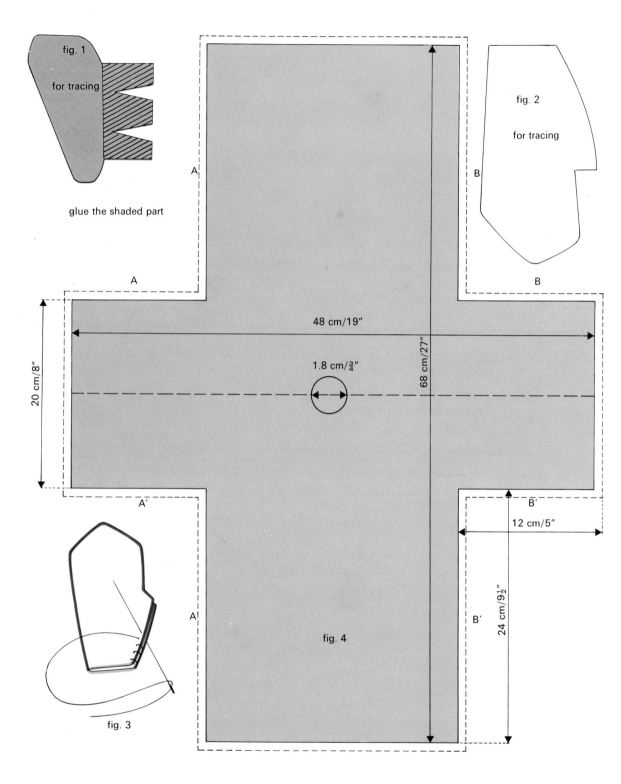

fig. 1

for tracing

glue the shaded part

fig. 2

for tracing

A

A'

A

A'

B

B

B'

B'

48 cm/19″

68 cm/27″

1.8 cm/¾″

20 cm/8″

12 cm/5″

24 cm/9½″

fig. 4

fig. 3

fold along the broken line
to sew sides and sleeves

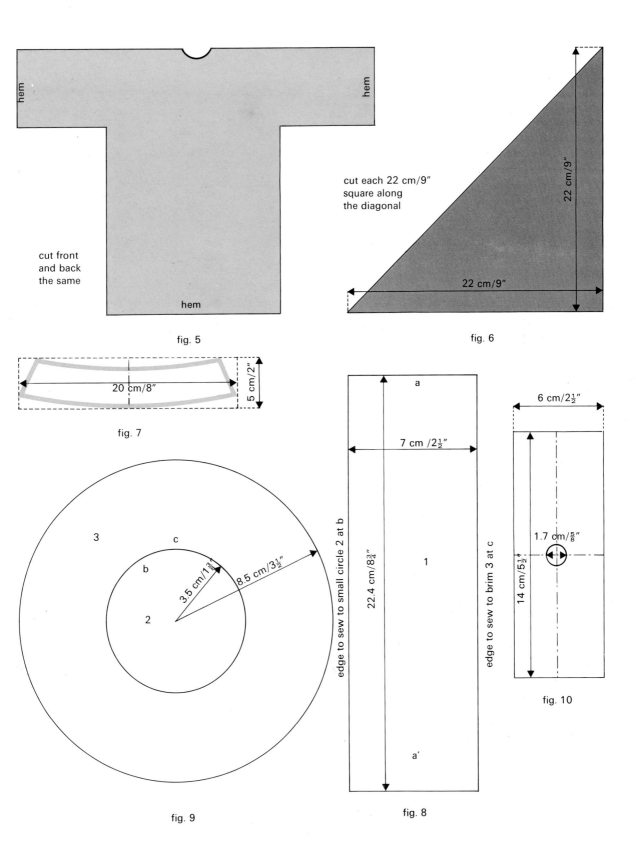

cut each 22 cm/9"
square along
the diagonal

22 cm/9"

22 cm/9"

fig. 6

cut front
and back
the same

hem

fig. 5

20 cm/8"

5 cm/2"

fig. 7

3

c

b

2

3.5 cm/1³⁄₈"

8.5 cm/3½"

fig. 9

a

7 cm /2½"

1

22.4 cm/8¾"

edge to sew to small circle 2 at b

edge to sew to brim 3 at c

a'

fig. 8

6 cm/2½"

1.7 cm/⅝"

14 cm/5½"

fig. 10

**Hands.** Following fig. 2, cut out hands in felt — pink for the hero and beige for the bandits. You won't need any extra for seams and hem, since felt doesn't fray. You need four pieces per person — four pink and 16 beige. Take them in pairs and oversew round the hand, following the red line. Stuff loosely with cotton wool and oversew along the blue line.

**Costumes.** Cut the shirts to the pattern in fig. 4 along the dotted line, leaving about 1 cm/ $\frac{1}{2}$" for seams. Sew A to A' and B to B', sides and sleeves. Gather the wrists and sew the hands into them. Put the rod part of the puppet through the neck of the shirt, and draw it tight with fine string on the inside so that it can't slip. Cover the bandits' necks with neckcloths cut to the pattern in fig. 6, and the hero's neck with a white collar (fig. 7). The hats are made of felt, cut to the pattern in figs 8 and 9 (pieces 1, 2 and 3). Join a to a' by oversewing. Attach the top 2 to the edge b also by oversewing, and the brim 3 to the edge c. To stiffen the shoulders, cut pieces of stiff paper 6 × 14 cm/ $2\frac{1}{2}$ × $5\frac{1}{2}$" with a round hole in the middle (fig. 10). Insert the rod into this hole and push the paper up towards the head to spread the shirt shoulders.

You can leave the shirts loose or hold them in with a belt of brown felt. The guns are made of strong cardboard.

Now the puppets are ready, and you can make up a play for them to act.

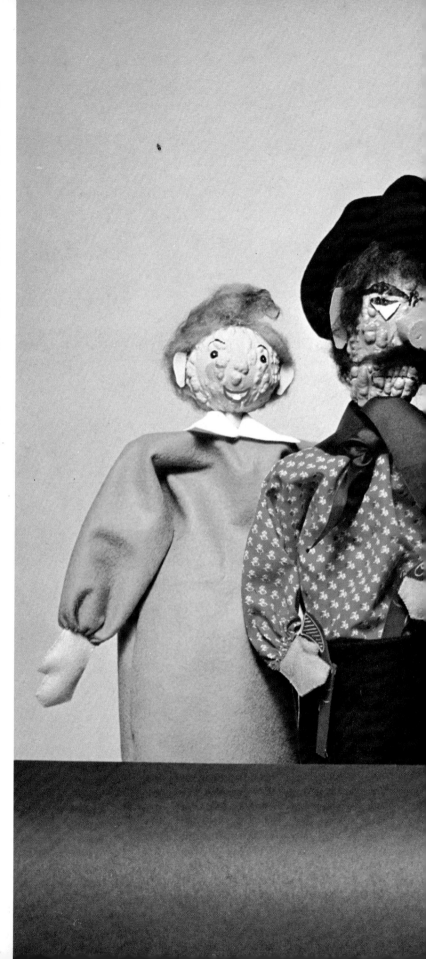